MW00857190

Homesick for Nowhere

Essays Inspired by Travel and Other Nuisances

Richard LeBlond

EASTOVER
—— PRESS ——
ROCHESTER, MASSACHUSETTS
www.EastOverPress.com

Homesick for Nowhere

Richard LeBlond

ESSAYS

ISBN 978-1-958094-05-1

BOOK & COVER DESIGN: EK Larken
COVER PHOTO: Richard LeBlond
BACK COVER PHOTO: Aija Briga

EDITOR: Walter M. Robinson

EastOver Press encourages the use of
our publications in educational settings.
For questions about educational discounts, contact us online:.
www.EastOverPress.com *or* info@EastOverPress.com

PUBLISHED IN THE UNITED STATES OF AMERICA BY

EASTOVER
— PRESS —
ROCHESTER, MASSACHUSETTS
www.EastOverPress.com

We do not take a trip; a trip takes us.

—JOHN STEINBECK

The bear was doing what a dozen gurus had failed
to do: bring me to total and continuous
focus in the present.

—RICHARD LEBLOND

CONTENTS

PART I.
ESSAYS INSPIRED BY TRAVEL
AND OTHER NUISANCES

PART II.
LIVING ON SAND

Part III.
Stories from the Outports of Newfoundland and Labrador

PART IV.
PAST REMEMBERING

PART V.
WRITING WHILE OLD

INTRODUCTION:
HOMESICK FOR NOWHERE

ZUMWALT PRAIRIE IS LOCATED IN THE NORTHEASTERN corner of Oregon between the Wallowa Mountains and Hells Canyon. It supports one of the largest buteo hawk breeding populations in North America and contains the largest bunchgrass prairie in the Pacific Northwest. Bunchgrasses get their name by growing in dense clumps rather than spreading out by runners.

The prairie is a nearly treeless expanse of low hills, plains, and swales. Wildflowers are abundant among the grasses, and in early summer there is an excess of color, as if some sloppy god had spilled his paints. The grasses sway not only to the wind but also to the scurrying of ground squirrels, badgers, and gophers, and to the predatory swoops of hawks and eagles.

At first sight, the fecundity seems to make no sense. The prairie is in the Wallowa Mountains' rain shadow, and the soils are too dry or rocky over much of the area to support forests. Grazing by elk and probably bison has also contributed to keeping the prairie treeless, along with fire. Euro-American settlers found the prairie too difficult to convert to cropland so put it under cattle hooves.

Elk continue to graze the prairie along with the cattle. The Nature Conservancy allows cattle grazing on its part of the Zumwalt but prevents large areas from being grazed in consecutive years, allowing habitat to recover. The Conservancy reintroduced fire in 2005. The combination of grazing rotation, fire-created nutrients, nitrogen-fixing plants, and life's tenacious ability to wrestle nutrition from the most meager soils has produced a marvelous diversity of plants and animals.

During my first visit, I saw one of the most beautiful and prolific wildflower displays of my life. About five minutes after I got out of the truck, a coyote started yipping at me from a low hill about three hundred feet away. He or she kept it up for about ten minutes; no doubt I was messing with its dinner plans. Corpulent ground squirrels were everywhere, and I kept stepping into badger holes— disconcerting, to say the least. It may have been impossible to scan the sky and not see a hawk or eagle. To the east, the prairie dipped down into the complex of gorges heading to Hells Canyon, and to the southwest I could see the snow-capped Wallowa Mountains over the shoulder of one of the Findley Buttes. And the wildflowers were stunning. As I got down on my knees to try and identify them, I spontaneously said, "This is home."

That afternoon, I went to the bookstore/espresso bar in nearby Enterprise to browse and hang out. During one of my brief conversations with the owner, I mentioned my experience on the prairie earlier that day. She handed me a chapbook titled *The Zumwalt: Writings from the Prairie*, a collection of essays, poems, and historical accounts. In an essay, "On Becoming Native to Place," by local resident Jean Falbo, I found a passage that deeply resonated with my experience on the prairie that morning:

> Before us was a herd of elk, perhaps two hundred animals. They stood tensely still, eyes on us and ears radaring in our direction. Some voiceless decision was taken and the herd moved down slope like a brown mudslide against the dark yellow green grass, gaining momentum as they went. A more distant herd on Findley Butte caught the

message and started its own slide over the undulating land and disappeared from view. A bright evening star appeared.

"This is *A'gamyaung,*" one of my friends, a Central Yup'ik Eskimo, said. After a pause, he went on to say, "It means 'I'm homesick for nowhere.'" Seeing we didn't get it, he explained that at moments like these, his people said, "*A'gamyaung,*" meaning *to be at one with the universe, no matter where one might be physically.*

Many of these essays were inspired by travel, especially to eastern Canada and the western United States. The lure of travel is irresistible, and not a day at home goes by that I don't think about resuming the adventure. Travel suits many strategies: escape, inspiration, knowledge, renewal, and self-discovery, to name some of mine, not all of which were anticipated. Travel is novelty, and novelty is rejuvenating. It tests what we already know and reveals strengths and weaknesses of character. Limits are learned, but they are also expanded.

Other essays here were inspired by time-travel to my formative years, particularly in the Pacific Northwest and Cape Cod. Time-travel increasingly becomes more suitable for my age, and aging itself has become an inspiration.

But in all of these modes of travel, it was the people I met who became the better part of the adventure.

Jean Falbo. "On Becoming Native to Place."
in *The Zumwalt: Writings from the Prairie.* Enterprise, Ore.: Fishtrap, 2008.

Part I.

Essays Inspired by Travel and Other Nuisances

Some of life's best experiences happen in
unfamiliar places, or from chance encounters,
or, as in the first essay here, from the cajoling of
others. Sometimes I have no fixed destination, which
exposes me to the "jeopardy of circumstance"
that William Least Heat Moon encountered
in *Blue Highways*.

Adventure and exploration thrive on uncertainty.

William Least Heat Moon. *Blue Highways.* New York: Fawcett Crest, 1982.

THE APPALLING MOUNTAIN

VICTOR HUGO SAID THERE IS "A SACRED HORROR about everything grand," and a mountain "seen too near, is appalling." I grew up near a grand mountain, Oregon's Mt. Hood, and I marveled at its sharp beauty the one or two days a year we could see it from Portland, when the clouds lifted their soggy skirts.

Up close that mountain is monstrous, all icy slopes, stone cliffs, jagged ridges, and avalanches of smothering snow. Steam spewing from its fumaroles is a constant reminder of its pedigree, a volcano dormant only since 1907, a blink of an eye in mountain time. Nothing lives up there except cyanobacteria, which are more likely to colonize Mars than we are. (We may have sent them there already.) But there are human visitors to the mountain who know that the higher up they go, the steeper it gets, and strenuousness becomes inversely proportional to oxygen. They are exhilarated by this prospect.

"Because it's there" is the most famous answer to the question "Why climb a mountain?" It is attributed to George Mallory, the English mountaineer who died on Everest in 1924 during his third attempt to reach the summit. There's a good deal of snoot in that answer, but it hides an underlying certainty that there is no other logical response. The answer is famous because we like its subtle arrogance. We wish the climbers well, but from a distance. Mountaineers are proof that logic is an acquired taste, easily lost.

Being a relatively sane man (and in regard to mountains, a wise man), it would never occur to me to climb
one just because we were both there. I have to be forced
or cajoled. I have never been forced to climb up a mountain, but I have been forced to climb down two. Once was
in the Navy in the 1960s, when I was a photojournalist on
a helicopter sent to rescue two people who had survived a
winter's crash of their small plane into the Cascade Range
east of Seattle. After the two injured people were loaded
onto the helicopter, there was only enough room for the
camera, and I was left behind on a snowbank. Happily for
me, a rescue crew was on its way up, but finding me in
place of the injured fliers was a great disappointment for
them.

The other time I was forced to climb down but not up
a mountain happened in Montana's Glacier National Park.
I was part of a wildfire crew sent into an area so remote
there were no roads or trails. Our helicopter landed on a
flat stony place above the tree line on the mountain hosting
the wildfire. We had to climb down through the fire to
fight it. (This event is recounted in the essay "Tea with the
Grizzlies.")

All of my other mountain climbs were the result of
cajolery and its powerful underpinnings: peer pressure,
competitiveness, and pride. Still, I have chosen my mountains carefully—or, rather, been cajoled fortuitously.

The most memorable and meaningful alpine experience happened on a mountain I needn't have climbed at
all, since a road goes right to the top. This is Mount Washington in New Hampshire's White Mountains, the tallest
peak in New England, though a mere footstool to those
overwrought monstrosities in the Himalayas. Somewhere
in the middle of the 1980s, I was talked into ascending
the ancient peak on foot by a good friend, Mark Primack.
Even now that he is in his seventies, Mark believes that re-

moteness and altitude, an unaltered view, the spicy smell of
conifers, a rill of Adam's ale straight from the brewery, and
wildflowers fragile at the time but jewel-hard in memory—
that all of these somehow justify the shredded ankles and
calves, the heaving lungs, and acceptance that the summit
is never going to be around the next curve or over the next
outcrop.

Mark guided me up Boott Spur along the mountain's
east flank, near Tuckerman Ravine. After a while, signs of
humanity had disappeared from view except for the trail
itself. Trees began to diminish in size and frequency, soil
was replaced by rock, and we emerged through an invisible membrane into another earth, one that exists above the
one where we left our routines. Parts of this other earth
can be seen from below, but not the whole. It is (almost)
pristine, where humans (almost) don't live and can only
visit. It is where the oldest mountains on Earth commune.
Deep down in the wooded valleys are the highways and
houses of lower earth, but they are hidden among the hills
and trees. It is a marvelous trick, this invisibility of human
construct.

The exception to this, the violation of upper earth by
the lower, is the tragedy of the summit. Mount Washington
is like a king whose half-billion-year-old crown has been
replaced with tinker toys and erector sets. The defiling
began in the middle of the nineteenth century, when two
hotels were built at the summit, creating one of the nation's
first tourist destinations. Shortly after, a coach road and cog
railway wormed their way to the summit. Weather obser-
vations began in 1870, and a meteorological observatory is
now manned year-round.

During the average year, though *average* is a concept
foreign to Mount Washington, 110 days will have hurri-
cane-force winds. A wind reached 231 mph on April 12,
1934, the strongest ever recorded on the planet until

surpassed by an Australian wind in 1996. Temperatures have dipped to -50 F, with wind chill values greater than -100 F. Annual snowfall averages more than 20 feet. With these bitter credentials, it has often been described as the site of the world's worst weather, though a prudent hyperbolist would confine the boast to the world's worst weather at a weather station. This "worst weather" makes Mount Washington one of the most dangerous and deadly mountains in the world.

Although not a tall mountain—the Rockies are more than twice as high—Mount Washington is perfectly situated on the cold side of the continent to catch Canadian-spawned storms, and the climate at the summit has been classified by science as subarctic. A blizzard can happen any day of the year. Spring, summer, and fall timidly dart about between late June and early September.

It was late June—early spring—when Mark and I reached the summit and found a miracle of wildflowers among patches of lingering snow. Cushions and carpets of magenta, yellow, and blue filled the spaces within a great disorder of boulders, jagged slabs of rock, and swaths of gravel. The wildflowers made no sense at all growing at the site of the world's worst weather. They were buried under ice and snow for nine months and blasted by howling winds the other three. They were making life out of the only thing the wind leaves behind: stone. How on earth could they live there, and if numbers count, live so well? Why would any life form "choose" to live in such life-threatening conditions?

Among them is a plant that grows only there and on one other subarctic New England summit, as if to say the weather just isn't bad enough anywhere else. It is Robbins' cinquefoil, a ground-hugging circle of tiny leaves, the entire plant no wider than a silver dollar. During our two days at the summit I spent too much time looking for this

flower, though it would have been just the right amount
of time had I found it. But during the search I came
across an object that gave some hint of why the brave little
cinquefoil was restricted to such a narrow and violent set
of conditions.

While meandering through a boulder field well away
from the nearest trail, I chanced upon a bronze plaque that
had been embedded in one of the boulders. It was a memorial to a hiker who had been caught in a blizzard at the
beginning of the twentieth century. The date of the blizzard
was June 30. Clearly the hiking life form was out of its
element, while the tiny cinquefoil, at full flower when the
blizzard hit, was in. The flower's strength was in its humili-
ty. It had conquered the summit by submission, prostrating
itself before the subarctic gods. The hiker, incompletely
acclimated, had been undone by his own upstanding
pride—or someone else's cajoling.

Robbins' cinquefoil could have been common in a
colder age when subarctic conditions held more ground.
The flower's brutal but beloved habitat may have been
abundant then and adapting to it would have made good
biological sense. But that adaptability can turn ugly if the
habitat shrinks. There may be no limit to the severity of
conditions life can master, but there is a limit to the number of conditions any one life form can endure, as the
hiker sadly proved. The cinquefoil is a master of adversity;
a kinder weather will kill it.

Mountaintops are full of mystery, as monstrosities
should be. During our last day on the summit, I awoke
early and headed toward an east-facing precipice, drawn by
a remarkable happening in the sky overhead. Clouds were
being made as I watched, formed and molded by invisible
hands. They looked like white smoke billowing out of an
enormous but invisible chimney. The new-made clouds
were speeding off to the southeast, yet immediately behind

them, in the same northwest wind, there were no clouds, just blue sky. I had never seen anything like it before or since. As I wrote this, my first inclination was to search the Internet and give the phenomenon sense, to know its mechanics, how the combination of temperature, humidity, and a clash between an updraft and a northwest juggernaut might have baked these clouds into being. But now, after a lifetime of trying to make sense, I am more interested in the mystery.

Victor Hugo. *Ninety-Three.* Trans. Frank Lee Benedict.
New York: Harper & Bros., 1874.

TOO LONG TEA

THERE WAS A CHOCOLATE SHOP IN THE TOWN OF Joseph at the foot of the Wallowa Mountains in northeastern Oregon. I visited the candy maker after discovering it was also a coffeehouse. Tea and a laptop would perfectly follow a morning in the alpine zone on Mount Howard. (The mountain has a tram to the summit, which is how my body, then in its eighth decade, got there and back in a morning.)

I asked the person at the counter what kind of tea they had. She waved her arm along an adjacent cabinet filled with maybe fifteen clear glass containers of loose tea, most with names I had never heard of.

"I have no idea which one to choose," I said. "But maybe you can solve an old mystery for me. I once had a tea that tasted like new mown hay smells, and I would love to have it again."

Behind the counter person was a large work area devoted to the store's main activity, the making of chocolate confections. Three or four women were working back there at large tables. The moment I posited my recollection, a strikingly beautiful tall, dark woman at the farthest table raised an arm. She looked Mediterranean, though I am holding out for *Nimíipuu* (Nez Percé). The woman wiped her hands on a damp cloth, came over to the counter, and asked a question that severed my anchor and set me adrift.

"Has the hay just been mown, or has it been lying on the ground for a while?"

As she asked her luminous question, full of portent and promise, she gently grasped my right hand between both of hers, our fingers extended. It was a surprising and intimate gesture. She couldn't have been more than twenty-five-years old. There was excitement, even a hint of breathlessness in her voice, as if we had set off on a wondrous adventure.

I would have robbed banks with her.

Somewhat less than fully conscious, I said the hay had been lying on the ground for a while. She brewed me a cup of Pingcha tea, which the Chinese normally ferment and age for five to fifteen years. But the batch she brewed had been aged for seventy-five years.

After I tasted it, I realized the hay had been lying on the ground too long. I should have asked for the just-been-mown tea, but that was now a minor point—except as a reason to return.

When she asked if it were the tea of memory, I lied and said the too long tea was the treasure I had been seeking.

In love and politics, truth is merely an option.

EATING AMERICA

I AM AN OLD ROADIE (EIGHTY-ONE AND COUNTING, WITH luck), and every summer I head west from my home in North Carolina. Roadside eateries are more than just food stops. They are the holdouts of the beefy high-carb meals fed to me by Mom at supper and Grandma on Sunday afternoons.

One recent summer, at the outset of a western voyage, I decided to eat regional foods wherever I was at day's end. I should have abandoned the project after the first day, as it was a lesson in American obesity. That evening, in Indiana, I asked the motel clerk if he could recommend a restaurant that served regional food. Maybe something from the German heritage.

He sent me to a "boiled chicken dinner" in Oldenburg, where all the streets are "Strasse." I envisioned chicken parts swimming in a broth, but instead I was served half a chicken that had been boiled—not in water but in a deep pool of oil with its one side dish, a bushel of french fries. From my seat at the counter I could see the vittles roiling in an iron skillet the size of a small swimming pool.

Next evening, in Amana, Iowa, I was sent to a restaurant run by the Ebenezer Society, a Germanic communal colony that settled there in 1856. Dinner was served family-style at large tables, where I was seated with perfect (and maybe a few imperfect) strangers. A steady stream of transporters brought plates and bowls filled with meats, breads, mashed and boiled potatoes, and side dishes of every vegetable grown in Iowa, what my grandparents called trimmings. Eventually, there were two large plates and seven bowls in front of me. And that was before dessert. In two days, I had eaten my weight.

Seated next to me was a Mrs. Weekley, fifteen years widowed. She told me she still had "his and her" tractors (I wondered whether this was a Midwestern pickup line), and that she got on the John Deere mower "whenever the urge arises" (and I stopped wondering).

Now that my stomach had been noticeably expanded, I figured I was ready for the Mountain G'oat breakfast in East Glacier, Montana, in spite of the awful pun. I was served a loaf of oats about the shape, size, and weight of a brick, baked with apricots, raisins, and egg ("for strength," said the waitress) and topped with a local huckleberry sauce. I think it is still lodged in my body.

Big helpings are the norm at roadside diners, and sometimes big helpings are taken to an extreme, offering a meal so large that if the eater can eat it all, it's free. I found such a meal in the middle of nowhere, Silver Lake, Oregon. The café served mostly ordinary fare—burgers and fries—but there were a few oddities, like alligator nuggets & fries, and a four-ounce gator burger for kids. I was told the gators were shipped from Louisiana "overnight," though the nearest airport was almost a hundred miles away.

On the wall behind the counter were six photographs of large young men. They were the ones who apparently believed their bodies were amusement parks and tried to eat the Double Big Hoss!!! It was a sandwich so large I think all of them must now be dead from ruptured plumbing.

Only one, a logger, succeeded in eating all of this vertical buffet. Between the halves of a six-inch bun were "2½ lbs. beef, ½ lb. bacon, ½ lb. ham, 6 slices each American & Swiss & ½ dozen eggs fried . . . GOOD LUCK!!!" Cost: $24.50, or nothing if you could eat it all. Weight: over

4 pounds.

I went for the health food: chili with onions and cheese, and a blackberry milkshake.

An Advanced Human Being

L OSING AN INTERNAL DEBATE, I HAD TO DRIVE MY
seventy-one-year-old keister from North Carolina
to Oregon in 2012 to spend Christmas with the
remainder of my family. Several friends agreed that it was
illogical. But I no longer like to fly and am running out of
Christmases. Although I drive to Portland every summer, it
had been years since I'd been to my old hometown for the
holidays.

I used to love flying, especially through the enchant-
ments of Cloud National Park. But the terrorists took all
the fun out of it, and nuisances of aging moved me from
the window seat to the aisle. Flying had become the equivalent of a giant elevator stuck between floors for hours at a
time.

Though it costs more and takes much longer, I love
being on the road, through forests and deserts, through
meatloaf and mashed potatoes at truck stop cafés. I took
the southern route to avoid Rocky Mountain snowstorms,
leaving early enough to give me a few days on the Oregon
coast.

It was late afternoon when I arrived at the coastal town
of Brookings, five miles north of the California border.
The area is known as Oregon's Banana Belt because of
the mild winters. *Mild* refers only to temperature; there was
nothing mild about that day's torrential rainstorm.

Tourism drives the economy of many coastal Oregon towns, but Brookings's economy is homemade: loggers, mill workers, fishermen, and prison employees. Notorious Pelican Bay, a maximum-security prison, known as "The Hole," is located just over the border in California. Charles Manson spent time there and has become part of local folklore.

I spent the night just up the coast in Port Orford. Next morning I headed to Paradise Cafe for breakfast. It was a workingman's restaurant. Like Brookings, Port Orford largely has an export economy, dependent on its own sweat. The Paradise opened at six, and at that hour there was just the cook on duty. He had to take orders as well as grill them. I was the only person sitting at the counter, but there were a few others seated at tables.

Then I noticed a man I had seen before, the previous summer, when my sister, her husband, and I had eaten breakfast there. After we left, we remarked about this man's appearance, part-laughing, part-mock terror, with allusions to the movie *Deliverance.* He had straggly long dark hair that hung over much of his face, blending into a beard of similar construction. The face itself was craggy, mean-looking, a face only a puppy might love, just before it was eaten.

And here he was again, sitting at a table with an older couple who, I was told by the cook, had just celebrated their sixty-fifth wedding anniversary. The long-haired man, maybe in his mid-forties, looked every bit as terrifying as he had the previous summer, the spawn of a prison hospital encounter gone horribly wrong, just across the border in California, begot by Charles Manson upon Nurse Ratched of *One Flew Over the Cuckoo's Nest*—or so I surmised from such limited data to work with. (I suspect all this is a tad politically incorrect, but it heightens the coming plot twist.)

While I was eating my breakfast, two men had a brief conversation with the cook as they were leaving to fish nearby Elk River for Chinook salmon. After they left, I asked the cook, "Are they commercial or recreational fishermen?"

"Recreational. I think the season goes until the end of January. Or maybe December—Eric!" he called out to the hirsute man, son of Chuck. "How late does the Chinook season go in Elk River?"

Eric reached into the inner depths of his cavernous black overcoat and pulled out what I half-expected to be a partially eaten puppy. But instead it was an iPad—a frigging iPad!—the device about a foot wide. Eric quickly found the answer, as he had already cached the data. After I recovered from this collision of universes, I said to the cook, "I don't even have one of those. He is an advanced human being."

"My words exactly," said the cook with gentle sarcasm and enough volume for Eric to hear. "He is an advanced human being."

With that, Eric smiled, got up from his table, walked to the counter, and sat down on the stool next to mine. We had a lengthy conversation that was amply illustrated with images from Google Earth. He was a placer miner for gold and platinum along Elk River. His workmate owned the claim, and Eric spent most of his time in diving gear. He stood on the bottom of the river with a hose, vacuuming gravel and sand—placer—out of benthic nooks and crannies. He was in the river for as much as an hour at a time, at depths reaching 20 feet. The hose transported the placer to the modern version of sluice boxes. The final sift was made with an old-fashioned miner's pan, winnowing the grit to its heaviest elements, the gold and platinum. The two precious metals were then separated with mercury.

(I was fascinated by Eric's account, as placer mining had been a hobby of my dad. But I am an environmental

biologist and must side with the river. Several states have
banned what is called suction dredging, and in 2013,
Oregon passed legislation reducing the number of permits
issued.)

   Eric told me he lived in a cabin along the river and
supplemented his income by filling his larder with fish and
game. That morning at Paradise Cafe, he railed against the
environmentalists, and I began to sense that mix of dread
and exhilaration a spy must feel. He railed even though
he legally hunted on land protected from development by
conservationists. That was not the only irony in the war
between protection and use. Eric was more intimate with
the land, more knowledgeable of its habits, and more dependent on its contents than the conservationist would ever
be. They faced in opposite directions, but their backs were
touching.

TEA WITH THE GRIZZLIES

I N THE EARLY MORNING OF SATURDAY, AUGUST 12, 1967,
two young women were killed by grizzly bears in Glacier
National Park. The killings took place in different areas
but happened within a few hours of each other. It was the
first time bears had killed anyone in the park's history, and
the two incidents led to a comprehensive national review and
restructuring of bear management on public lands.

Though the killings were not directly related, odds argued
against purely coincidental events. Garbage was determined to
have played a role at one site, and campers' food at another.
Lightning strikes were also considered as a possible influence.
That night, more than a hundred ground strikes had been
observed by fire lookouts in the tinder-dry park. By Saturday
evening, thirty separate fires had been reported, and crews
were already fighting thirteen of them. It was, and maybe
ever will be, the most terrible day in Glacier's history. (Those
interested in learning more about the bear killings should
read *Night of the Grizzlies* by Jack Olsen. A strong stomach is
required.)

The months of July, August, and September of 1967 were
the driest in fifty-three years of record keeping at park headquarters in West Glacier. By the end of the fire season, thirty-five fires had been fought and suppressed inside the park,
with the number of acres burned greater than in the previous
thirty-one years combined.

August 12 marked the beginning of a war. The park
shut down its normal operations, and tourists were kept out.

Most able bodies joined fire crews. Park wives and secretaries operated around-the-clock dining halls. The Forest Service supplied smoke jumpers and aerial tankers (retardant ships), while the Air Force provided helicopters. Native American fire crews flew in from reservations as far away as New Mexico and Alaska. I was sent to a fire so remote we had to be flown in by helicopter and let off on a ridgetop in Canada.

I had arrived in the park that May after successfully applying for the entry-level position of personnel management specialist. Within a day or two after Saturday's wholesale incendiary, I was assigned to the crew that would fight what became known as the Gardner Peak Fire. It was in a remote wilderness very close to the Canadian border and the Continental Divide, above Upper Kintla Lake. There were no roads or human trails to the area. The attack team consisted primarily of two Native American crews, one from Zuni Pueblo in New Mexico, the other from a tribe in Alaska. Each crew had the manpower equivalent of an army platoon and was divided into squads. Although the hierarchy of the unit was theoretically based on government job qualifications, the actual hierarchy was based on tribal structure. Discipline is more easily achieved when the chief is the foreman. It echoed the contrived structure of the park's own management, where the majority of supervisors—superintendent, division chiefs, and their assistants—were former World War II Army officers.

The Gardner Peak Fire had started on the south slope of a mountain whose summit was in Canada. Because of the remoteness and difficulty of access, we were brought in by troop helicopters to the mountain's summit, a flat-top ridge. From there we hiked down rocky escarpments, across unstable scree slopes, and *through the fire itself* to reach the unburned area below it. The fire was only smoldering at the moment of our audacity, but red coals were launched as our boots scudded through the ashes. While crossing the avalanche-prone scree slopes I wondered what I had gotten myself into, and in the coals I found out. As in war, the individual life had to cede its value to the cause.

Our first task on reaching the valley floor below the fire was to build a base camp. This included construction of a small landing platform for a two-person helicopter. The troop helicopters that had brought us to the top of the ridge were too big to service the base camp. The plan was to have the larger helicopters drop off supplies on the ridgetop in Canada, with the smaller copter shuttling from ridgetop to base camp. That plan went into effect the morning of the next day, and I was chosen to be airlifted back to the top of the ridge to assist in the unloading of the larger helicopters and the loading of the smaller one. The small helicopter lifted me to the nascent alpine supply depot about midmorning. The pilot then flew off to the staging area closer to park headquarters, after telling me he would return with the larger helicopters. He was gone a while, and then a while more. In fact, I did not see him again the rest of that day. I was on the verge of a strange interlude.

It was sunny, and for the duration of that day I likely had one of the most spectacular views of anyone in the world. I was at the southern edge of Akamina Ridge, most of which is in British Columbia. Well above the tree line, my companions were the neighboring mountains, Upper Kintla Lake, and small ridgetop glaciers sitting in their cirques. I had a lunch and was dressed warm enough for daytime conditions in an area that freezes every night of the year.

While waiting for helicopters, I made short forays into the adjacent alpine habitats. An Alaskan would know this place well, with its ice-carved topography and gravel beds sparsely peppered with ground-hugging arctic plants. The day wore on to late afternoon, and I began to think of other things—about why the helicopters had not returned, about food, about nightfall, and whether I had been forgotten. Most of all, I tried not to think about bears. Grizzly bears. It was only a couple of days after the horrors of August 12.

I was in what was more and more becoming part of primary grizzly bear habitat. In our conquest of the continent, we had driven the grizzly out of the plains and foothills and higher up into the mountains. It had reached the realm of the mountain goat. This top predator will even kill and eat a black bear.

The beauty around me began to fade, not only from the sun's descent but also from my predicament. I was without options. My fate was entirely in the hands (or paws) of others. I had no food, radio, weapon, or nighttime insulation, and was probably the most frightened I had ever been. Would the grizzly find me warm or frozen? The value of my life seemed to have bottomed out.

I tried not to dwell on what had happened to the two young women who had been mauled and killed. But I had already seen the results of a bear mauling, on the face of a young man who had come into my office in West Glacier. He had been mauled by a bear when he was a boy, and his face looked like it had been put back together by Picasso. It was difficult to look at him yet impossible not to, like passing a car wreck.

Even worse for my consideration was the face of one of the park's naturalists. It had been burned when a prairie fire he was fighting had quickly reversed direction. His face had burned off, and he was now, in 1967, several years into its reconstruction from other parts of his body. He needed frequent surgery just to remove hairs growing inside the flesh that remained where his face had been. Even his ears were gone. Yet here he was, working every day, and in the summer interpreting the park's resources for the tourists. He had their rapt, morbid attention and might have been the most important thing that happened to them that trip, whether they knew it or not. Because of his public exposure, he had to frequently retell the story of the worst moment of his life. I could not resist asking him either. He told the story calmly, seemingly even willingly. Three months into my park service career, I was growing up quickly.

Then the sun set, and I was truly and righteously afraid. I figured I could not possibly have been forgotten, so for some reason I had been abandoned. It must have been a humdinger of a reason.

And then I heard a low rumble in the direction of the Kintla lakes. It was the most beautiful sound, the engine of the helicopter that was bringing back my life. It was one of the larger copters, and it landed on the ridgetop about a hundred feet from me. I thought it was going to pick me up and take me somewhere, but instead it had brought provisions. And what provisions they were—a sleeping bag, a tent, enough food to feed eighty people for a week, and the schoolteacher who was going to cook it.

We unloaded the helicopter, and it returned to its base of operations. The cook told me the cause of the delay was a logistical problem involving the food supplies, but he didn't know what that problem was.

Among those supplies was a crate full of Lipton Tea. I later learned that after I had been airlifted to the ridgetop, members of the Alaska fire crew went on strike, refusing to man the fire lines until they had their cups of tea. I was never able to confirm that the psychological adventures of that day were spawned by an emergency tea run, but the evidence argued that I (and a portion of the burning forest) had been among the strike's collateral damage.

With what little light was left, the cook and I set up the tent, built a fire, and ate like kings. Next morning, the supply helicopters arrived early, and my life returned to normal on a ridgetop in Canada that was apparently too high even for grizzly bears.

Jack Olsen. *Night of the Grizzlies.* New York: Putnam, 1969.

RIDING IN THE BACK WITH KILLER

THERE IS A GOOD REASON WHY YOU MAY HAVE NEVER heard of the sixth largest island in the West Indies (after Cuba, Hispaniola, Jamaica, Puerto Rico, and Trinidad), North Andros in the Bahamas. Although it borders a sea trench, there are no deep harbors at island's edge, and the cruise ships go elsewhere. That leaves its emerald waters and white sandy beaches to those who prefer to create their own itinerary in paradise. For me, it was three botanical expeditions in the early 1990s to North Andros, with meals and lodging on the beach at Miami (Ohio) University's Forfar Field Station, now closed. I was accompanied on all three journeys by one or two other botanists from the States.

Greater Andros Island is a collection of many islands crowded together, and North Andros is larger than the rest of them combined. The distance from the north end of North Andros to the south end of South Andros is more than a hundred miles. North Andros itself is nearly seventy miles long and forty-five miles wide at its broadest. The sparse human population is almost entirely of African descent, with many tracing their ancestry to people who had been freed from slave ships by the British during the early 1800s. They were deposited on the island rather than returned to Africa. The original inhabitants, the Lucayans, had been completely wiped out by slavery and disease by 1520. *Lucayan* derives from the native Taino phrase meaning *people of the islands* and is the root of the British *cay* and American *key,* as in Key West.

North Andros is the water supply for the Bahamian capital, Nassau, located about thirty-five miles to the east on the island of New Providence. It is one of the smaller islands in the Bahamas but has deep harbors.

On our third expedition to North Andros, in 1993, we arrived by commercial flight from Ft. Lauderdale on a plane so small that one of the passengers sat next to the pilot. The Bahamian government required that the field station transport its guests from the airport by local taxi. When the guests departed, the taxi again had to be summoned. But in between, we didn't have to use the taxi at all and never did.

Our taxi on arrival was driven by a large, good-natured woman who sang for us with a very fine voice. I told her we were interested in hearing some traditional island music and she said there was a "rake and scrape" band playing that night in Nicholls Town at the north end of the island. With six hundred people, it was the largest community on all of Andros.

As we neared the field station, our driver invited us to come to her church to hear some gospel music. "Come any night but Wednesday," she said. She told us Wednesday was the night the preacher drove the devil out of everyone, and all of that disembodied evil gathered into the most sinful person in the building. Her warning was generous, but I had a nagging feeling that behind her kindness was a simple certainty that the most sinful person would be among us.

Although my sample size is small, religion with a touch of the old ways strongly influenced their lives. One of the field station's researchers told me about an incident when she was helping in the kitchen, where a few local women were employed to do the cooking.

"I see you are left-handed," said the Andros cook to

the researcher. "That means you owe something to the devil."

"Owe what?" asked the researcher.

"You'll know when you get there."

Andros Island is noted among herpetologists for the endangered Andros rock iguana, which can reach three feet or more in length and has a large orange head. In spite of the iguana's endangered status, the animals were being killed on sight during the time of our visits and then eaten. I was told they weren't being killed primarily for food, but because they were reptiles, kin to serpents. To the Androsians, extinction would be a blessed achievement.

Most of the island's people seemed to be getting by on a subsistence economy rooted in home gardens and in what could be gathered from the ample sea. The pace of life was slow and idyllic, at least for the men. During the day, women seemed mostly to stay home and tend the gardens while the men gathered in groups at a small and remote convenience store, or along the main road at places where a vehicle had just died. Repair and replacement parts were apparently unavailable or unaffordable, and the gatherings were essentially wakes. Every now and then, a government bulldozer would push the car-casses (sorry) off the roadside and into the adjacent woods. We eventually realized there were scores if not hundreds of shrub-enshrouded dead automobiles in the woods along both sides of the road.

Meanwhile, back at the remote convenience store, sales were slow in spite of the crowd, but that was just our perspective. A field station researcher told us that one day she brought a van filled with about ten students to the small store for sodas. The proprietor shooed them out and closed the door, telling them they were too many people to deal with.

This economic pace also governed the island's few

restaurants. Before heading to one for dinner, it was necessary to call first. Otherwise, it wouldn't be open. Or if it was open because someone else had called, you still couldn't eat. There was only enough food for those who had called ahead and placed their order for the inevitable two choices: chicken and conch. The field station may have had the most reliable kitchen on the island.

After dinner that first night a group of us headed north in the station's pickup to hear the music in Nicholls Town. About halfway we encountered a man hitchhiking, a popular form of transportation on the island. Our hitchhiker was none other than James "Killer" Smith, lead singer and shaker (of maracas) for the Potcakes, Andros Island's only rake and scrape band. He acquired his nickname while working as a policeman in Nassau. I know of no other place where it would be comfortable to ride in the back of a pickup with a hitchhiker nicknamed Killer. He was enthusiastic about our interest in the music, and when we got to the club where his group would play, he introduced me to Kelly, the group's guitarist. Kelly appeared to be at least a generation older than the other musicians. Much of what I learned about rake and scrape was told to me by him.

Rake and scrape music has two roots: goombay and junkanoo. Goombay is Bahamian calypso and gets its name from the conga-like goombay drum. Junkanoo is a festival surviving from the days of slavery and is related to the John Canoe festivals of Jamaica, Haiti, Belize, Bermuda, and—of all places—where I live, eastern North Carolina, where they were recently revived after not having been celebrated since the 1800s. The Junkanoo Festival takes place on the mornings of Boxing Day (December 26) and New Year's Day. It features fancy costumes, a procession, and percussive music of cowbells, horns, whistles, and goatskin drums—the goombay drum, open at one end. Periodically, procession participants stop and light fires to heat and tighten the drums.

Rake and scrape is basically calypso music with a Junkanoo rhythm section. The most important percussion instrument is not the goombay drum but the carpenter's saw, which today is raked and scraped with a table knife or screwdriver. The original scrapers, dating back to the nineteenth century, were spoons on washboards or sticks on animal jawbones. According to a historical account, these were replaced in the 1920s by the bottle and nail, featuring the corrugated bottle of Gilby's Gin during the smuggling heyday of U.S. Prohibition, and by the carpenter's saw with nail, knife, or screwdriver, arising from the Nassau tourism construction boom occurring at the same time.

According to Kelly, rake and scrape music was a dying art form in the Bahamas in 1993, too primitive for Nassau tastes. He thought there were no more than five bands left. Kelly said Cat and Long islands were the heart of rake and scrape, where it was strictly acoustic and played around a bonfire at night.

The Potcakes did not immediately strike the ear as a polished band. Kelly's electric guitar was out of tune by at least a quarter-tone for the entire performance. I now think this may have been intentional, an exaggeration of the slightly flat tuning of the guitar by Joseph Spence, a well-known rhyming singer. Spence was from Small Hope, a town about fifteen miles south of the Forfar Field Station. At the time of our visit he was living on South Andros Island. In his guitar, the off-tuning produced a blues-like undertone. The blues in Kelly's version was not in the guitar but in the pain to unaccustomed ears.

Killer sang too loudly when leading, and he was the electrified lead singer. Most songs featured a volume imbalance among individual musicians—and for the discerning listener, an unusual use of pitch and cadence.

At times, each musician seemed to be playing to a different drummer. Nonetheless, the music was very lively, often compelling, and in a few instances, particularly in a song titled "Cat Island," transcendent. I don't know what happened for "Cat Island," but suddenly they were very polished musicians, in balance and in time during a lovely song. Even Kelly's guitar seemed momentarily in tune. I think the well-played songs were the ones they had played most often, and they just needed more practice (possibly a lot more practice) on the rest. The difference was so great that if I had only heard and not seen them, I would have sworn the songs were played by two different bands. My guess is that they were not able to practice at all and could only perform. The other musicians were the sawyer, a bass guitar player, and the goombay drummer. The sawyer cradled the saw between his hand and shoulder and bent it to produce different tones.

While we were there, the commissioner of North Andros came in and sat down with us. He reminded me of one of those suave tropical characters from a 1940s Bogart or Mitchum film, but with a better tan. After a while, he sat in with the band for a few numbers, playing a second saw. Quite possibly, we were listening to the world's only band with a saw section. Unlike the band's regular (or first) sawyer, he placed the end of his saw on the floor to bend it and produce the different tones while scraping. The commissioner told us he knew Joseph Spence (who died in 1994, the year after our visit), and that his music was a combination of Bahamian calypso (goombay) and gospel. He said Spence played the guitar as if each string were a different instrument, the effect being that the guitar seemed to produce more music than its innate capability would suggest.

We had no idea that we'd be hobnobbing with the island's chief government official, let alone that he would be a player of and expert in the indigenous music. I wanted to repay his kindness, but as usual I impulsively tested the waters.

"Would it be graft and corruption if I bought you a drink?"

He paused, gave me a hard look, then smiled and said, "You can buy me a drink."

MOORINGS

O CRACOKE IS A SMALL AND ISOLATED FISHING VILLAGE on the Outer Banks of North Carolina. It has so many sophisticated attributes that I refuse to relate them for fear you will discover this place, tell others, and—like me—trample its charm underfoot. I fell in love with the first person I met, Patricia, who conveniently happened to manage the hotel where I had my reservation.

This story is about Patricia's daughter, Denise, who was in her early twenties and also living in Ocracoke, but not in the hotel. Denise was accompanied everywhere by a mongrel dog that sort of resembled a black spaniel. If Denise was sitting, the dog was curled at her feet. If she was working, it was sitting or lying nearby, with a constant eye on her. It tolerated other people, but there was no one else it cared about, no one else it greeted when they entered the room. I had never before met a dog so attached to one person. (I am not counting those living toys found in Gucci handbags, and a shame to wolves everywhere.) Denise was perfectly content with the attention.

Daughter and mother were headstrong, and they occasionally fought. These were mostly verbal fights that quickly devolved into a traditional airing of each other's faults. Objects were occasionally thrown, sometimes damaging or destroying family heirlooms. But overall, this was an improvement in their relationship.

An attractive young woman, Denise had gone to Hollywood after high school, where the driver of her dreams shifted from stardom to drugs. She entered an abusive relationship, and her life descended so low that her mom was able to convince her to come to Ocracoke. The detoxification period was hard on both of them, but after a while Denise made a few friends, got her own apartment, and began participating in local activities. She fell in love with sailing and eventually acquired a small sailboat.

The village of Ocracoke occupies a low area near the southwest end of the island. This lowness gives rise to what I consider the village's only drawbacks: mosquitoes and flooding. The many freshwater and brackish wetlands are mosquito nurseries. The "dry" land is so low and flat that streets are flooded after ordinary rainfalls with puddles large and deep enough to tempt canoes. You don't want to be in Ocracoke during or immediately after a hurricane. The whole village floods. Patricia had sent me pictures she had taken from the second floor of the hotel during one hurricane. The first floor was under water.

It was during a hurricane that Denise had a reckless and life-changing encounter with her sailboat. As usual, the town flooded from the storm surge, with rainfall adding to the ruination. Denise had an apartment on the second floor of a house along the sound. From one of her windows she had a view of her boat, which was moored close by. Nearly continuously, she monitored the steadfastness of the mooring and considered possible mishaps that might occur as a result of the storm surge lifting the boat above what had been land. There was in fact nothing now but sea between her building and the boat.

A hurricane is a terrible thing while it is happening, and just when you think it can't get worse, it does. Denise became so concerned that the boat would come loose from its mooring that she decided to examine it up close, in the hurricane, in the rain, in the storm surge—and out of the relative safety of the apartment. This is how people die in hurricanes. She was in water before she reached the bottom of the apartment's stairwell. In the flooded yard between her and the boat, the water came up nearly to her knees. The walk was slow and treacherous in the choppy water and strong winds.

When Denise got to the boat, she determined that the mooring was secure and turned back toward her apartment. About halfway, she heard within the noise of the storm what sounded like the distant, muted yowl of a dog in pain or fear. Scanning the environs, she thought the sound might be coming from a nearby small one-story guesthouse. As she walked toward it, the yowls got louder. She approached the window that seemed closest to where the sound was coming from. Looking through the window, Denise saw the water was more than a foot deep in the little house's kitchen, and still rising.

In the middle of the room was a table and leashed to one of its legs was a mongrel dog that sort of resembled a black spaniel. The dog was straining uselessly against the table and rising tide, more thrashing than swimming, and no doubt knowing it could drown. Then it saw Denise through the window, and its yelping took on precious new meaning.

After determining no humans were present, Denise tried the front door, but it was locked. So she grabbed a piece of floating wood and burst through the kitchen window. Climbing inside, she untied the dog from the table leg, picked it up in her arms, unlocked the front door, and carried the dog out into the storm. By now the surge was up to her knees, and the dog began to squirm upwards. It was trying to get up on her back and shoulders, farther away from the water, so she let it. Then the two of them set out for the safety of her apartment.

The cottage guests who had so carelessly abandoned the dog never attempted to find out if it survived the storm. Denise didn't try to get in touch with them; they had forfeited their rights.

Patricia noticed almost immediately the calming effect the dog had on her daughter. Denise said it was fated, that it could not be more obvious the two of them belonged together. It might seem trite to say each had given the other a priceless gift, but each had.

Let's Restore the Draft

O THER THAN ME, THERE ARE NO VETERANS AMONG blood relatives in my family. I had the good fortune to serve between two wars: Korean and Vietnam. Back then, our wars were sequential instead of pop-up targets. No one in my family has had to experience what it is like to have a relative at war. But my sister's husband, who joined our family in the 1990s, is a twice-wounded Vietnam vet. Although I was against that war, I was never against the veterans who fought it.

At the time, there was a draft. In a stroke of seemingly unsurpassable callousness, the government turned one of the best days of the year for a young man into a death lottery. If your birthday was the first one randomly drawn, you were the first to be drafted. Consequences of avoiding the draft included imprisonment.

Vietnam veterans took the heat for a war declared by civilians. The My Lai Massacre and slogans like "Kill them all and let God sort them out" didn't help. But war begets brutality, demands brutality. Who can say what a man will do when others are incessantly trying to kill him? The battlefield has its own morality.

The treatment we gave to returning veterans was shameful. Many were scorned or shunned, as if the war were their idea. The government fell well short of what was needed and deserved by returning veterans and their families. They received substantially fewer benefits than returning World War II veterans. The Vietnam veteran was spurned even by those who sent him to war.

I am a retired biologist living in eastern North Carolina, not far from Camp Lejeune Marine Corps Base. I moved to the area in 1990 and have worked on the base. During that time I have gotten a glimpse of the relentless burden suffered by the families of active service men and women.

In some ways the government has made no progress at all. After stonewalling for decades, Congress finally granted compensation in 2012 to veterans and family members sickened by water pollution in Camp Lejeune. But to pay for the compensation, Congress raised the interest that veterans pay on certain home loans, as reported by Tom Philpott in *Stars and Stripes*. In other words, the veterans are paying for it themselves. (Speaking of unsurpassable callousness . . . .)

A few years after 9/11, I was surveying habitat on Camp Lejeune with one of the military installation's biologists. At the time, her husband was a helicopter pilot in Afghanistan, and I asked her how she was dealing with it. She replied calmly, even though what she said was harrowing. It was part of her daily life:

"I can't have the TV or radio on at home, and I try to avoid places where they are on. I freeze every time the war is mentioned, afraid they'll report there are casualties. I can't help but think my husband will be among them. Worst of all is when I hear a car slow down outside the house, afraid they have come to tell me he's been killed. That happens almost every day."

Then there are the children. Marines returning to Camp Lejeune from deployment in war zones sometimes surprise their offspring in televised encounters. I don't know whether it is the military, families, or TV stations that trigger these surprise visits, but the children have no idea their war zone fathers have come home. Surprised preschool children usually run into Dad's arms laughing. But school-age children are more likely to be bawling their heads off. That is because they have lived every day with classmates whose fathers (and even a few mothers) can never come home.

These conditions are a constant for every partner, parent, child, and sibling of every service man and woman at the front.

I have a proposal that may reduce the number of our sons and daughters killed in battle, reprioritize motivations for going to war, and send spin doctors to respectable employment. It involves a partial restoration of the draft.

No troops can be sent into battle until all age-eligible children and grandchildren of every U.S. senator, congressperson, and White House staffer (including POTUS) have been drafted into combat units. Next on the list are the age-eligible children and grandchildren of family units with current annual incomes of $400,000 or more (the "one percenters"), as these families have enormous influence on the politicians.

I think it would make a great constitutional amendment. We could even require they be drafted on their birthdays.

Tom Philpott. "'First Step of Justice' for Ailing Camp Lejeune Vets." *Stars and Stripes.* August 9, 2012.

ALTERNATIVE DEFINITIONS

NO COLLECTION OF DEFINITIONS CAN ESCAPE THE shadow of the mother of irreverent lexicons, *The Devil's Dictionary,* by the alphabetically inclined Ambrose Bierce. (I am going to take a break here to see if I can compose a twenty-six-word sentence that begins with "Ambrose Bierce" and ends with "Yankee *Zeitgeist.*") The mostly nineteenth-century American author may be best known for his legendary disappearance into Mexico in 1913 to lend a hand (and maybe a life) to the revolution.

Bierce collected and saved his micro-epiphanies for decades, beginning at least as early as 1869, and holding on to them until the 1911 publication of his devilish dictionary. I have done something similar (though on a far smaller scale), tending them carefully over the decades, with an eye for drooping vowels and smudged consonants.

They seem to arrive out of nowhere, often with great fanfare—unbidden but not unjudged. Those that continue to shine in daylight are bathed and swaddled. Some claim to be a clever insight, or a punishing twist, or, as Bierce said of bigamy, "a mistake in taste."

AUTOBIOGRAPHY. An exercise wherein an author determines which lies to tell and which truths to leave out.

AUTOPILOT. It appears to get stupider as we age, but in reality it has always been this stupid and is merely getting more airplay.

BASEBALL. A game in which 98 percent of the time is spent watching two men play catch.

BOOT CAMP. The mechanism by which the soldier is relieved of his common sense.

BUFFET. A cafeteria freed from tyranny.

CHARISMA. An aphrodisiac that works in both directions.

CHURCH. A car wash for the soul.

CORNAGE. Every comedian's nightmare.

COSMETIC. Makeup is not so much about of the superficiality of women as it is about the superficiality of men.

CROTCHETY. Rejected term for PMS.

DEMOCRACY. An indulgence of generals.

DYXLESIC.

ECONOMIC GROWTH. The communists and capitalists have more in common with each other than either has with those who would live in a sustainable way.

ELDERLY. When normal is the new euphoria.

EPOCALYPSE. The destruction of evil is taking longer than predicted.

FREEDOM. A term that now is more identified with restrictive political and religious beliefs than with personal liberty. It is becoming its own oxymoron.

FREE ENTERPRISE. The mechanism by which capitalists achieve a monopoly.

GOD. A metaphor for all that remains unknown or unexplained, enabling us to imagine causality in the interplay of physical laws and the chaos of chance. God as an entity is unknowable except for one thing: everything.

HONEY. We are repulsed by the thought of insects in our diet, but we love to eat their vomit.

JUNK SCIENCE. (1) Scientific studies contrived to support a point of view; (2) any scientific study, contrived or otherwise, that does not support your point of view.

KISSING. An ingenious device of our immune systems, whereby we share our defenses with loved ones. Science has determined that as many as eighty million bacteria are transferred during a ten-second kiss.

LOVE. An ingenious device of bacteria.

MATURITY. Women don't fully mature until around age 27, whereas men are fully mature by age 12, or just before puberty.

MEANINGLESSNESS. A luxury of youth, and a worm of old age.

MIRACLE. Something with a 10,000-to-1 chance of happening. No one noticed the 9,999 times that it could have happened but didn't. Our mind abhors randomness and attributes a cause to every effect.

MISSIONARY. The name for the most popular form of sex in the world. They must be very proud.

MNEMONIC. A word sorely in need of its own service. Minnesota (MN) will have to do.

MUSIC. The first language, far more emotionally complex and subtle than words could ever be.

ORGANIC FOOD. Not intrinsically good. An organic spaghetti Alfredo means your heart attack is more likely to be cancer-free.

PACIFICATION. One-word oxymoron. (See *freedom.*)

PATRIOTISM. It freed us from the British but hasn't freed us from ourselves.

PEACE. Euphemism for the interlude between wars, always and only a morphing regional phenomenon.

PENANCE. Only as good as its beginning. That which begins with a crisis of conscience is of great value. Much more common, and essentially worthless, is that which begins with getting caught.

POETRY. The soul's shorthand.

PORK. Tax dollars going to someone else's district.

RACISM. It is from children we learn that racial prejudice does not come naturally and has to be taught.

RESPONSIBILITY. When something you need to do but don't want to do goes to the top of the list.

ROUTINES. Vain and futile attempts to make time move sideways instead of dead ahead.

SARCASM. Aggression cloaked in humor, the crudest form of rapier wit. It descends from a Greek word meaning "to tear flesh like dogs." No kidding.

SCHOOL. An ingenious cultural convention whose primary purpose is to train the citizen to show up on time five days a week, whose secondary purpose is to educate, and whose tertiary purpose is to prepare the citizen for war through athletic rivalries.

SOAP OPERAS. With someone furtively listening outside an open window or behind a door in nearly every scene, these should have been called "eaves droperas."

SPECIAL INTEREST. Any interest not special to you.

SPOONING. A mildly amorous position that nonetheless can lead to forking.

SUICIDE. Dark cousin of our noble capacity for self-sacrifice, and maybe the cost of that capacity.

SUNSET. Misnomer for earthrise.

TATTOO. A lifetime commitment often mistaken for a lifetime commitment.

WELFARE. Sometimes people need to be rescued from forces beyond their control. And sometimes people need to be rescued from the rescuing.

XENOPHOBIA. The ultimate expression of our immune system.

IN AN OKINAWA KITCHEN

THERE IS A RESTAURANT IN JACKSONVILLE, NORTH Carolina, that is staffed by several women from (or descended from) the island of Okinawa in Japan. Jacksonville is the home of Camp Lejeune, the largest Marine Corps base on the East Coast. The Marine Corps has a strong presence on Okinawa, so it is not surprising that some Okinawans and their descendants now call Jacksonville home.

The small restaurant has two seating areas: a few tables out front and a counter in back that forms one side of the kitchen. I am an American of European descent who loves sitting at the counter so I can watch and listen to the women as they cook and transport Okinawan lunches. Accents are strong, especially among the older women, and sometimes I wonder whether they might be speaking Japanese or even the Ryukyuan language of older Okinawa. I assume that at least some of the younger women were born in the United States, and their accent was learned at home. That is how band leader Lawrence Welk got his German-accented English. He was born and raised in a rural Germanic community in North Dakota.

I am writing this at the cusp of age eighty. Though fraying at the edges, the center holds. Because I am now solitary and living the life of a suburban hermit, I am often slow to pick up on newer tenants and nuances in the Age of Behavior Modification, of political correctness and its inevitable plunge into censorship—oops! I mean cancel culture.

I grew up in an era that thrived on political incorrectness. It is imbedded in my unconscious and is the home of many incorrect but instinctive responses in social situations. I recognize that these responses are not the fault of my conscious mind, but it is my fault to knowingly let them lie there uncorrected. With great effort over extended time, I have learned to intercept some of these incorrectnesses before they exit my pie hole and cause harm to me or others. Political correctness requires constant vigilance.

So back to the Okinawa kitchen, which prompted this examination. I know I'm not supposed to make much—or anything—of physical differences, but that's not the human default. Noticing physical differences is. The Okinawa women on average seem darker than those on the islands to the north, which are in the temperate zone. Okinawa is subtropical. Hotter climates require more melanin for protection against solar radiation.

My racist upbringing feasted on melanin. When I was growing up, even southern Europeans from Portugal to Italy were suspect because of their African proximities and ties, and their own higher natural levels of melanin. I remember the politically incorrect culture questioning the racial correctness of Lucille Ball's husband, Desi Arnaz, who was from Cuba, where the races seemed more compatible.

Our capacity for demeaning others, whether by racial or cultural characteristics, is ancient and universal. When I lived in Montana, we told North Dakota jokes. It has occurred to me that the demeaning is the ultimate expression of our immune systems, keeping us alert to, and away from, strangers from strange lands. There of course is a biological basis for this: consider the decimation by disease of Western Hemisphere indigenes during the European invasion and conquest.

In the COVID-19 pandemic we were quick to blame the Chinese for something that might have happened anywhere. According to recent research, the Spanish Flu of 1918–20 most likely originated in North America, with the earliest-known cases in Kansas and New York. All we know for sure about the origin of COVID-19 is that it was first documented in China. Ultimately, it doesn't matter where it originated. We Euro-Americans will continue to disparage other races and cultures—that is the default, the form; melanin and virus origin are just content.

In war, demeaning others isn't enough. We must demonize them to justify killing them. To this day we call the conquest of the West the Indian Wars because it is less morally complicated to kill enemy combatants than it is to kill people defending what is left of their homeland. In war, racism and ethnicism become patriotic.

Given their deep human history and universality, racism and ethnicism will be impossible to eliminate by willful behavior modification alone, as so much of it remains invisible to so many people. It will be interesting to see how much applied political correctness—authoritarian behavior modification—we can accept.

PART II.

LIVING ON SAND

Many of these essays are among the more than one hundred that were first written between 1986 and 1990 for the Cape Cod Museum of Natural History in Brewster, Massachusetts. They appeared as a nature column, "Naturalist's Notebook," in four weekly newspapers: *Cape Codder, Falmouth Enterprise, Provincetown Advocate,* and *Yarmouth Register.* Where appropriate, the essays have been updated for their appearance here. Their subjects are as relevant now as when they were first recorded (too often, sadly so).

During my time on Cape Cod, I was variously an administrator for an environmental organization, a seasonal naturalist at Cape Cod National Seashore, a botanist for the Center for Coastal Studies, a bookkeeper, and director of a local land trust.

LESSON AT THE FEEDER

THERE WAS A TIME WHEN I WAS CONTENT TO BE A fair-weather naturalist. As soon as the arctic days of winter arrived on Cape Cod, I set up a small market of bird food just outside the picture window and let nature come to me. There, in the comfort of a roaring oil furnace, I could add to my bird list while buttering toast. It seemed a contender for the best of all possible worlds.

This notion was reinforced by the Titmouse Coincidence. It was the winter of 1969 and Massachusetts Audubon had announced a tufted titmouse census for a February weekend. I had just moved to Cape Cod from the Pacific Northwest the previous October and had yet to see the titmouse. By February I had already downgraded the chickadees, juncos, and blue jays from novelty to riffraff. I needed new blood. This possibly best of possible worlds could become a bore.

Thanks to the titmouse, it didn't. This bird of muted color and beautiful form was apparently an avid reader of Massachusetts Audubon bulletins, because it arrived at my feeder on the morning of the first day of the two-day census. Alternatively, maybe the bird world had called for a census of feeders for that same weekend. Whichever, I took the credit on behalf of humanity, happily filled in my sighting postcard, and wallowed in the glory of my first contribution to New England science. Best of all, it had happened as I sat at the dining room table.

Like the mourning doves and blue jays, I became a

bird feeder junkie. Nearby trees were festooned with mesh bags of suet and peanut butter. Thistle seed was added to the main feeder, which was nothing more (nor less) than the surface of a picnic table and the ground beneath, where seeds had fallen through the cracks in the tabletop. I also had hung from trees a few of those feeders designed for small birds only, but even the small birds fed most frequently at the tabletop, between the blue jay shifts. It was a wonderful time, those first encounters with dickcissels, redpolls, and grosbeaks. My bird list pencil was smoking.

I never found out if my second winter could have held a candle to the picture-window perfection of the first. Before that first winter ended, an event took place that shook me out of that contentment, and out of the house. I don't remember how much time had passed since the titmouse census, but there was still snow on the ground, except under the picnic table. My habit then, when home during daylight hours, was to sit at the dining room table facing the picture window. This way my attention didn't have to be fixed continuously on the feeders. (My bird-watching habit was not quite that obsessive, nor nearly that scientific.) I relied on the movements of the birds in my visual periphery to alert me to new arrivals, thus enabling me to engage in other sedentary pursuits. It was in this setting that the life-influencing event occurred.

It was late afternoon and daylight was dimming. While sitting at the table reading a magazine, three bobwhites arrived in my periphery. They had just landed under the picnic table to feed on the seeds that lay on the bare ground. By then bobwhites had become a dime a dozen, so after giving them an obligatory two and a half cents' worth, I returned to the magazine.

And then it happened. Suddenly, there on the picnic table stood a red-tailed hawk, its foreboding aura filling up the picture window. For a few endless seconds we were

five frozen creatures: actually, one frozen and four poised.
The three bobwhites, genetically equipped to deal with this
situation, had already arranged themselves for the Russian
roulette escape ritual. When alarmed, a feeding or sleeping
flock of bobwhites will fly off simultaneously but separately
toward roughly equally spaced degrees of the compass.
The visual effect is that of a rapidly expanding circle and
has been described as a feathered bombshell. Since a predator can only catch one victim even if all the bobwhites fly
off in the same direction, the full-compass takeoff is probably meant to startle or confuse the would-be diner.

The hawk was looking straight ahead, its back to me.
We were both facing south. The bobwhites, not designed
to keep destiny waiting, burst out from beneath the table. One flew east and one flew west. Due south, about
50 feet from the table and 60 feet from me, there was an
explosion. The snow, instantly littered with feathers, turned
red. I sat transfixed and watched the red-tailed hawk eat
its bobwhite. Several minutes passed while the hawk ate,
and I experienced a reasonable feeling of culpability. I had
taken *bird feeding* to an unexpected level.

Afterwards, in the dying light, I went out to inspect
the carnage at a ragged crater in the snow. My mind was
filled with the image of three bobwhites beneath the picnic
table, of the one that flew south, of ritual and violence. As
I stood there, nothing moved or made a sound. Yet nature
was vibrantly alive, even in death, in the blood and feathers
at my feet. I looked where I had been sitting in the cozy
warm light behind the picture window. The hawk had
taught me that even there I was a participant. Nature could
never again be just a pastime.

AMPHIBIOUS ASSAULT

IT HAS BEEN RAINING HARD FOR SEVERAL HOURS—NOT
your typical summer drizzle, but a forty-day-forty-night
special. Tonight, there will be no reading of newspapers, no fidgeting with the bills, no dining in a cozy Cape
Cod restaurant. Instead, I will drive the amphibious assault
craft, for this is the night that has called forth the toad and
the toader.

I was conscripted for the work by a good friend who
is studying the eastern spadefoot toad, a creature about
whom very little is known. Our ignorance of the spadefoot
is not due to a lack of interest, but to the peculiar lifestyle
of this biological relict. It is more closely related to ancient
lost tribes of amphibians than it is to any living family of
frogs and toads. The spadefoot apparently spends the great
majority of its life below ground, emerging only on wet
nights, probably to feed, and on the wettest to breed.

The spadefoot is equipped with a hard and pointed
tubercle on each of its hind feet, which is its "spade" for
burrowing into dry soil. A descending spadefoot takes with
it a lungful of air, burrowing to a depth as great as three
feet, and remains there until called out by a summer down-
pour. It is thought this self-entombment can last as long as
several years. On one breath.

The toader and I have been out before. There has been
a full cup of rainy days this summer. We saw spadefoots up
and down the Outer Cape, scattered and solitary, but out
and about. The problem with these earlier forays was the

lack of a breeding rain.

The spadefoot only breeds in temporary pools and puddles because they are fish-free. The pool or puddle has to be deep enough to allow time for the transformation from egg to tadpole to toad before the nursery disappears. Although many breeding attempts end in dehydrated failure, the spadefoot has the miraculous ability to make the transit from egg to toad in two weeks, clambering out onto land with its tail still evident, ready for a life of mostly sleep.

Driving the amphibious assault craft is not an easy task, because it is on the road itself where the toads are first found. The driver is always in danger of squashing the project, and of presenting a hazard to other drivers on dark and rainy nights. The toader and I agreed from the start that the main highway, Route 6, was off-limits to the study. Only on the side roads can this modern assay of ancient urge be effectively and safely employed.

The Outer Cape is so small and the road system so extensive that crossing asphalt barrens has become part of the journey for the toad venturing from upland woods to bottomland puddle. For some reason, both the common Fowler's toad and the rare spadefoot halt on the asphalt. Maybe they sit soaking up the surface rainwater or are disoriented by the flatness and hardness of the roadbed in what is otherwise a journey of humic descent. Maybe they sense something alien or are stymied by a silence in the genetic code. Whatever, there they sit on the road, looking like small stones or, too often, medium-size pancakes.

"Toad!" shouts the toader, and I bring the craft to a stop. It is a spadefoot. Down go the windows, in spite of the rain, and we listen. But the road toad is not the quarry. It is the indicator. We are listening for the breeding pool.

The spadefoot has the strangest mating call of all our toads and frogs, but we rarely get to hear it. This call has

been described variously as a coarse low-pitched complaint
from a young crow and a deafening roar—agonizing, hoarse,
and woeful. The toader and I had listened to recordings of
this call and were prepared.

We had been prepared all spring and summer. After
hundreds of miles of stopping for toads and toad-like rocks,
sticks, and oak leaves, we wondered whether we would ever
hear the call in the wild. So far, all we had gotten for rolling
down the windows at each spadefoot sighting were rain-
splattered laps. But this night of heavy rain—possibly the best
spadefoot breeding rain since the launching of Noah's Ark—
had potential and did not let us down.

The voices of what turned out to be three lovesick spadefoot males made their way up an embankment through the
sheeting sound of the rain. (For what it's worth, I'll add my
own description of the spadefoot mating call: it sounds like a
sick duck.) We worked our way down the embankment and
found the toads clinging to rushes in a pool maybe six inches
deep. With a flashlight we were able to watch this lonesome
trio, the vocal sac expanding to three times the size of the
head before each croak. The sudden release of air caused
their little bodies to bob up and down on the submerged
rushes.

We returned three days later to see if the male spadefoots
had found romance. But instead of finding eggs or tadpoles,
we found a waterless mudhole. Somewhere up the hill, the
toads had snuggled themselves once again into the Cape's
soft earth, to endure what likely may be another fruitless
summer. There they will wait out the seasons and the years
as they have done since parting with the ancients. They spend
so little time on the Earth and so much time in it, the greatest threat to spadefoots is not a dried-up pool or the asphalt
barrens but the unearthing of their foundations for our own.

SAND LOVERS

I N THE EARLY 1980s I WORKED AS A SEASONAL
naturalist for Cape Cod National Seashore. Among
our daily duties in the summer of 1983 was a two-hour
shift at an area called the Sand Bowl near the Province-
town/Truro border. It had its own parking lot and was the
only area in the park where people were allowed to scram-
ble up and down the face of a naked, migrating sand dune.

This popular but highly erosive activity was scheduled
to be shut down for good at the end of the 1983 season.
Our job as naturalists was to explain to people why the
Sand Bowl was going to be closed to the public, and why
a fence had been erected along the summit of the dune.

We made use of the fence to explain the closing. It had
been erected the previous year to keep people from using
the Sand Bowl and its parking lot as a means of getting
into the dunes proper, or for walking all the way to the
Atlantic beach.

Over the years this use had created a series of footpaths
that crossed several dune summits on the way to the beach.
These paths had created lines of exposed sands through
the vegetation. Erosive blowouts—the beginnings of new
migrating dunes—had developed on the windward faces of
some of these dunes at the trail sites. The fence at the Sand
Bowl greatly reduced trail traffic but had not eliminated it
altogether. Some people still broke through the fragile fence
or trampled it down.

But the fence also served another purpose familiar to

old-time Cape Codders. Actually called a snow fence, it
was made of thin wooden slats wired together and standing
vertically. In winter along the highway, the fence caught snow.
But in the dunes, it caught blowing sand. There was so much
blowing sand at the Bowl that the four-foot-high snow fence
was almost completely buried after one year of catching sand.
Its barely exposed top spoke volumes, and a new fence had
to be erected.

We naturalists used this handy evidence to highlight the
sensitivity of the area, and the fact that the Sand Bowl's particular dune ridge was migrating into adjacent Pilgrim Lake
(now East Harbor) at the rate of about 20 feet a year. Most
visitors grudgingly acknowledged the need to close the Bowl.

One day I had the morning shift at the Sand Bowl. The
first task on this shift was to climb the nearby higher dune,
Mt. Ararat. From its vantage, we scanned for dune trespassers
and then scanned the snow fence on the Sand Bowl summit
for trespass damage. I recall neither trespass nor damage that
morning, as all earlier memory was erased by the sight of the
couple making love at the base of the fence.

"Oh, no," I groaned. Though I wore the park service
uniform, I'm not really the law enforcement type, and didn't
look forward to this encounter.

But I quickly realized I had no choice. At that moment,
from my high vantage, I saw that a family group was walking
up the face of the Bowl and heading in the direction of our
sand lovers.

I figured I had less than two minutes and ran down Mt.
Ararat toward the snow fence. As I approached the couple—
still at it, by the way—I slowed to a fast walk. They neither
saw nor heard me until I passed within two feet of them.

"You've got about forty-five seconds before Mom, Dad,
Grandma, and the kids get here."

Ancients among you will remember that old TV game show *Beat the Clock*. These two would have been great contestants. The family group never knew what it missed.

Almost immediately, the family and I entered into a discussion of the Sand Bowl's erosion problems and its imminent closure. Our now-vertical lovers slowly edged their way into this discussion and even asked a few polite questions. When it ended, the family walked away, but the couple hung around. The two of them wanted to thank me for a double lesson, one on erosion and one on the effectiveness of the mellow reprimand.

The site of this event is now covered with planted beach grass, whose Latin name, *Ammophila*, means "sand lover." The players have changed, but the passion remains.

BIGFOOT

*This essay was first drafted in June 1988, just after the incident
it describes. It concerns the imperilment of the piping plover, a
small beach bird that has been on the U.S. Endangered Species
List since 1986. It continues to be imperiled as of this updating.*

THE DAY HAD BEEN SCHEDULED FOR COLD AIR OUT OF
Canada, a lousy way to start up June. But by the
time we had gathered at the parking lot near the
beach, the wind had died, the sun had punctured through
those cold Canadian clouds, and we were treated to one of
those fabled "What is so rare?" June days.

The beach belonged to a town on Buzzards Bay in
Massachusetts, and our group included two members
of the local conservation commission, a piping plover
researcher, a citizen "activator," and me. A few hundred
yards down the beach, up where the berm above high tide
blends into the toe of the fore dune, a pair of piping plovers had scooped out a small pocket in the sand and laid
the customary four eggs.

These two sparrow-size birds and their nest had
reached a statistical significance wholly out of reason. But
these are unreasonable times.

There were seven breeding pairs on this beach in 1986,
but in 1988 it was down to two. That had been the trend
since monitoring began in 1983. In 1987, there were 126
breeding pairs of piping plovers in all of Massachusetts, the

largest population within any of the political subdivisions of the Newfoundland-to-North Carolina breeding range of this federally protected species. The whole Atlantic Coast population was estimated to be no more than seven hundred pairs.

During our walk down the beach I was introduced to the particulars of this town's fore-dune system by the citizen activator. He knew where every blowout and overwash had happened, even though the scars had been healed by new beach-grass ridges. And he knew when and how many piping plovers had nested in the old scallops and hollows of blowout and overwash.

Unassuming and always smiling, he knew things would be set right again in some eon just around the corner. His information was infused with a quiet but dogged love for land and sea. I understood why one of the conservation commission members had said he was "an activator, not an activist." He knew how things worked, from fore dune to town meeting, and had learned to work with them.

A fortress of rope and warning signs had been erected around the plovers' nest. It was risky, calling attention to the site like that. But the alternative was worse, and that was soon apparent.

"There she is," said the plover researcher, scanning the nest site through her binoculars from our vantage point about a hundred feet away. The female plover had scooted off the nest and was standing about three feet from it, so I was told. Looking through my own binoculars, I scrunched my eyes into X-ray mode and still couldn't see her, even though, as it turned out, I was looking right at her.

The piping plover has a distinctive black band around the neck, and another black band across the forehead from eye to eye. The rest of the body is the color of dry sand.

In spite of the distinctive black bands, the bird as a whole presents what ornithologists call a "visually disruptive pattern." When a running piping plover stops, it disappears.

The four eggs are even less visible in their nest of sand. But it is in this perfect mimicry that another danger lies.

The piping plover was a "hat bird" shot nearly to extinction for the millinery trade around the beginning of the twentieth century. When that practice was outlawed, the bird made a strong recovery into the 1940s. The present decline began shortly after World War II with the rapid development of residences and recreational beaches along the Atlantic coastline.

Every year, some piping plover nests and their youthful contents are naturally lost to storm tides and overwash. Animal predation is on the increase from a mixed bag of natural and human-influenced causes. The adults will usually replace a lost nest. Four nesting attempts were recorded for one pair at this beach in 1986.

Habitat has declined. Gulls, profiting from our wastes, have overrun plover breeding sites. Natural predators such as raccoons, skunks, and foxes have also increased in number at the beach because of our edible wastes. Pets, especially unleashed dogs, add to the toll.

On top of all this is Bigfoot. The perfect mimicry of plover eggs on the beach has turned against itself. At this Buzzards Bay site in 1986, twelve of fifty-two eggs (23 percent) were crushed by unknowing human feet.

The wall of rope and signs strung around the nest of our visit would improve this pair's odds. There are far more clumsy and unknowing bigfoots among us than there are vandals, though one vandal can undo it all.

The little lady standing invisible inside her human-built fortress needs all the help she can get against the tides she cannot see.

Rooming with a Weasel

I MET MY FIRST WEASEL IN A CAPE COD DUNE SHACK. That should be of little surprise to anyone familiar with weasel behavior. This small mustelid related to martins, otters, and skunks rarely builds its own house. It most frequently nests in abandoned rodent burrows. If the desired home is still owner-occupied, the weasel draws up a quick and tasty deed transfer.

Not having to acquire an undeveloped lot saves the weasel plenty of time and energy for the pursuit of its main mission, the daily consumption of up to 25 percent of its body weight in the form of small mammals, birds, snakes, and frogs.

To the weasel, the dune shack is just another burrow—a bit large, but with roof and walls, usually abandoned, and in good habitat. The shack in which the encounter occurred differs from other shacks I am familiar with by having a second room. This room is largely occupied by a double bed, also uncommon among dune shacks. Solitude is not merely available. It is encouraged.

I had finagled a week's stay in this shack and arrived with a mule-sized load of goods without benefit of the mule. I set out my food and belongings—a scent in every corner—and inspected the shack's own store of provisions in the outer room. Food, of course, is mighty important when shacking it, and one must always bring a complete set of edible weapons for the war against starvation (actually, against the long, difficult, and should-have-been-unnecessary walk back to the grocers).

Former tenants can be expected to leave something edible. Some things everyone leaves: marginal items like herb teas and tamari sauce, and staples like rice and powdered milk. And rancid items like the bacon I threw out and the greasy Oriental noodles I kept in, deeming the former dangerous and the latter useful in a dangerous time.

During this sorting of ported and inherited possessions, the time came to put my sleeping bag and clothes in the interior bedroom. I opened the door and—wham!—the weasel encounter.

Already on the bed was an abandoned sleeping bag. Instantly, my eye caught the movement of something in the bag. Suddenly the weasel stood one-foot high on its hind legs, staring at me with an expression that seemed half-surprise and half–sizing up. In a moment it had flowed—that's how a weasel moves—off the side of the bed and through a small hole in the floor. The encounter lasted less than three seconds.

After a suitable wait, I gingerly pried open the sleeping bag to see what—or who—might still be in it. There among the flannel folds was a thick, soft nest made of the hair of one of the dunes' more popular rodents, the meadow vole.

On the outside chance the weasel would return, I decided to sleep in the outer room, which had a bed of its own. It paid off. The weasel, willing to share, continued to use the other room, and I saw it fleetingly two more times during my stay.

Following that first encounter, I returned to the ordering of possessions. I couldn't believe it when I opened a kitchen cabinet and found a nestful of newborn, juvenile, and adult white-footed mice. It seemed unlikely that the weasel (whose spine is so supple it can make a U-turn in a soup can) had not found this overpopulated nest. Could this have been the weasel's larder? Had it, like me, stashed its belongings here and there?

Of course not. This was a case of incredibly lucky mice. One peep too loud and they would be nest upholstery. Weasels do not husband livestock.

Weasels kill livestock. This is what has given them such a bad name. In spite of their small size (they average less than half a pound in weight) they are fierce fighters and can easily kill animals several times their size. Like any successful natural hunter, a weasel will kill more than it can eat at one meal. If it makes its way into a rabbit's burrow or chicken coop, it will kill everything in sight, eat what it can, sleep it off, then eat again. More than one weasel has come to an end fast asleep inside a coop of dead chickens.

On Cape Cod, rodents are the primary diet. Weasels themselves are prey for foxes, larger birds, and even house cats. But the sinuous animal can be a very ungrateful dinner guest. The skull of a weasel was once found with jaws still clamped to the breast of a live eagle.

THE NATURAL MOMENT

THIS HAS BEEN AN UNUSUALLY BUSY WINTER FOR ME. What used to be a given—a daily walk in the outer Cape Cod woods—has become a luxury. There is meager compensation from being too busy to fret about it.

But prolonged absences can make us more receptive to what is known as the natural moment. This is a sudden, unexpected event, such as an encounter with an animal or a sound out of the blue. It is a moment that has the form if not the content of revelation. The mind is instantly ushered from its internal rumination to a state of external awareness. It is a wake-up call.

One recent night I took our dog outside for his last chance before bed. It was a calm night, warm for early spring, and not a cloud in the sky. While the dog frantically searched for that perfect place, I sat down on the bench we had rescued from a junk heap at a Hyannis pond. It was while sitting on the bench that I was hit broadside by the natural moment.

As so often happens, the moment was generated by a sound. It was neither a loud nor a sudden sound and had been there all along, unnoticed. It crept up behind and leaped into my awareness, and for a few moments I experienced a state of higher consciousness, a mind disconnected from its preoccupations and reconnected with the world around it. It was one of those moments during which a sense of time and place is simultaneously pinpointed and obliterated.

The source of the sound was the ocean, specifically, the sound of heavy surf on the outer beach two miles away. The previous day we had been visited by a nor'easter, and though the wind was gone, the storm's stored energy continued to thrash the shore. The sound of the surf, though distant and of few decibels, was nonetheless huge and primal. It was a sound I had heard many times before, but this time there was something in it that seemed out of ancient memory, a sound originally heard from the other side of the surf, from within the sea.

The natural moment was further elaborated by the arrival of a second sound, that of a foghorn. There was no need for a foghorn on such a clear and windless night, and I fancied that this sound, like the waves, was a product of yesterday's storm, disconnected and tossed about, a false hope for a lost mariner.

Not all sudden or unexpected sounds result in the natural moment. Some produce the unnatural moment, and these most often are of human origin, usually mechanical. Nowhere is one entirely free of them. Even in remote wilderness, airplanes can be heard or their vapor trails seen.

But origin is relative, and whether a stimulus is mind-expanding or annoying isn't always determined by whether it was produced by nature or by humans. The nearest I have come to prolonged experiences of only natural sounds has been during lengthy stays in a dune shack. Yet one of my favorite sounds in that solitude happens at night, under the quilt, listening to the distant putter of fishing boats. They sound like giant faraway butterflies with piston-driven wings.

A wondrous mockingbird provided my favorite dune moment. The bird was on the other side of a cranberry bog, in a beach plum thicket. I was only partly listening to it when it mimicked the call of a Fowler's toad. That caught my full attention, so I sat down on the lower slope

of the dune on my side of the bog. This bird did each call
twice, then went on to the next. He focused on the dune
aviary, but allowed the occasional shorebird and mimicked
another dune toad, the American. But his tour de force
was not a natural sound at all. He perfectly captured the
muted sound of a semitruck passing on Route 6 a mile
away, immediately followed by the passing of a second
truck. Then he continued with his accounting of the dune
aviary. After that, a mile-away truck became one of my
favorite sounds in the dunes. It had become the call of a
mockingbird.

But back to the foghorn we left adrift a few moments
ago. It and two cohorts were responsible for another of my
favorite natural moments on Cape Cod. It was an August
day in 1974, after I had just returned from a two-year
absence. I was standing on the low bluff that sits between
Village Pond and Cape Cod Bay in North Truro, refresh-
ing my memory. I was wondering why the foghorns at
Race Point, Wood End, and Long Point were sounding on
such a clear day when all of a sudden the three of them
bellowed at once.

For those of you familiar with such things, it was
in more ways than one a major chord. I later asked our
resident composer about this phenomenon. He too had
become familiar with the foghorn tones, though he had
never heard them in unison. He described the three tones
as a second-inversion A-flat major triad.

The most distant horn was eight miles away, meaning
that a very large area was momentarily bathed in a rich,
harmonious music. It had all the earmarks of the best
natural moments: unexpected, coincidental, and mind-expanding.

The Coast Guard employs a foghorn tuner. It is his
job to make sure each horn has a distinctive tone for iden-
tification. I just had to call him, and he said the major triad

(second inversion) was unintended. He has since rescored the music to a dissonant chord, also without intent. That's as it should be. Part of me would have loved to hear that huge music again and again. But the memory of the moment would have been lost in the repetition.

Rough at the Edges

I WAS OUT AT THE BEACH, LOOKING FOR A "LOST" COLONY of seaside bluebells, a subarctic plant whose southern-most outpost is on Nantucket. But it was not a good day for botany—or botanists. After two hours of combing a Cape Cod National Seashore fore dune, I had found nothing but twenty-seven tons of beach grass and beach pea, and a Fowler's toad. There was, however, one area I couldn't search, a missing tooth in the combing where I am sure the bluebell hides, accidentally protected from human incursion by a squadron of terns.

As usual, I was walking with my head down, about 30 percent of my awareness devoted to not crushing clumps of beach grass. I had completely forgotten about the terns, in spite of having been attacked by them during a futile bluebell search the previous year. My memory was quickly revived by a piercing alarm. I looked up to see a feathered missile descending toward my head with its wings and legs held outwardly from its body. At the last moment it arched over and dove for my scalp. I ducked in time but felt the wind of its wake.

Within moments another half-dozen terns had joined their companion and the battle intensified. In self-defense, I flailed my hat at each dive by these small terrors. I stumbled hurriedly through the lumpy beach grass terrain, crushing clump after clump. I had made a mistake and the fore dune was paying for it. Never walk through the backyard of a tern nesting colony.

I know of no bird that displays as much physical threat to humans during nesting as the tern. The blackbirds may outnoise them, but the blackbird is only bluff (so far). The tern will back up its threat with a sharp peck to the head or by unloading an organic bomb from its aft gunnery. Anyone who experiences this attack comes away with a grudging admiration, but often at the cost of lost affection. The tern is a good example of Henry Beston's observation that wild animals "shall not be measured by man. They are not brethren, they are not underlings; they are separate nations."

One of the more difficult aspects of nature for us to accept is the differing "morality" of behavior between wild animals and ourselves. This happens because we too often judge such behavior not on what seems right or wrong for the animal, but on what seems right or wrong for us. The parental tern provides a good lesson on the inappropriateness of this attitude.

The tern chick and fledgling are preyed on by a host of two-to-six-legged creatures. These include gulls, hawks, snakes, foxes, skunks, and rats. Even ants will enter the cracked shell of a hatchling and kill it. But the predator posing the greatest threat to terns on Cape Cod is the great horned owl, which attacks at night in eerie silence. The owl is therefore a threat to the adult terns as well as to the young. Because of this, the adults abandon the nesting colony at dusk and spend the night offshore. They won't return until dawn. The chicks and fledglings spend the night alone and unprotected.

Judged by human standards, this behavior would rate two-inch headlines in the tabloids, the parents would be in jail, and the children would be wards of the state. But in the nation of terns, the adult is paramount. The balance of behavior tilts, as it should, toward survival of the species. For an interim, you can have adults and no chicks, but you

can't have chicks and no adults. Orphaned chicks are wards
of the fox. If necessary, adult terns will produce more than
one brood in a season.

After my own recent scrape with the terns, I continued my search for the wayward bluebells. In another
quarter-mile I found myself at an area of the outer beach
reserved for off-road and recreational vehicles. As I approached close to the vehicles I overheard a boy about
eight say, "Dad, there's a man walking in the beach grass!"

"I know, son, I see him."

"Shoot him!" the boy said.

Although I had coated myself with false innocence
during the first part of this conversation, I blew my cover completely when I involuntarily laughed at the boy's
concluding statement. He was right of course: not that I be
shot, but that people aren't supposed to walk in the beach
grass. Beach users are strongly warned about this in the
national seashore. My special dispensation to find the bluebells was not apparent and in any case did not cover what
I did to the beach grass behind the tern colony.

The boy's suggested method of righting my wrong got
me thinking about the terns again. I was glad I could take
the father's civility for granted, but were the codes of our
separate nations so separate after all? The terns would have
no trouble accepting such a ruthless solution. Maybe our
discomfort with ruthlessness in nature is in response to our
own capacity for violence.

TRESPASSING FOR FUN AND PROFIT

SOMEONE WHO REGULARLY ENGAGES IN AN OUTDOOR activity beyond one's own yard—nature walker, hunter, beachcomber—often becomes a petty criminal. The crime is trespassing.

Outside of Cape Cod National Seashore, most of the open land on Cape Cod is privately owned, as is most of the beachfront down to low water. For obvious reasons trespassing is more of an issue these days. We all want our privacy, even if at the expense of someone else's, whether trespasser or trespassee. Trespassing is nothing if not a tradition. Our ancestral recreationists were even guiltier than we are today, but in those days there were far fewer encounters with the owners of the land, and the crimes for the most part went undetected.

This raises an interesting point about the law. Generally, one is not apprehended for trespassing on private undeveloped land unless the owner complains. In effect, one trespasses against the person, not the land.

I am a professional trespasser. My habitat research work for a state agency requires that I walk private land. When possible, permission of the owner is first obtained by letter, phone, or in person. But sometimes this is not possible. A case in point is a survey I conducted of rare plant habitat at about a hundred Cape Cod pond shores during the summer of 1985. This peculiar habitat is only exposed during periods of below-average water levels, and sufficient exposure only happens about once every five years.

Since this exposure is directly related to annual and seasonal rainfall, it is almost impossible to predict when exposure will occur. There is no lead time within which to contact the thousands of landowners at the one hundred ponds, assuming one has the budget and personnel to pay for the contact effort.

So one (that would be me) ignores the Keep Out sign and prays for civility. Technically, the law covers this research by permitting egress on undeveloped private land for state natural resource surveys. But such niceties of the law tend to inflame rather than reassure many landowners. Illegal trespassing may be bad, but legal trespassing is worse.

Many—and rapidly becoming most—of our pond shores are ringed with houses, and all want a view of the pond. The pond shore surveyor thus is an easily noticed disturbance and develops a sixth sense for looks from house occupants, looks that are charged with suspicion or apprehension. I learned quickly that the best way to approach these encounters was to immediately identify myself, explain the nature of the work, and request the occupant's permission for continued but brief trespass.

With one exception, this has always worked, and some-times worked wonders. Many pond shore residents are delighted to hear they own part of a naturally significant habitat. Some have registered their land with The Nature Conservancy in a legally nonbinding moral commitment to help protect the pond shore. During one encounter, I was served cranberry juice and homemade chocolate chip cook-ies, then invited to speak at the local garden club. Send for my book on trespassing for fun and profit.

Then there's that one exception, which is good, because it keeps me from growing complacent, and provides essay fodder. I was surveying a pond in the mid-Cape area that was rimmed by a formidable wall of highbush blueberry, except where homeowners had cut a swath to the shore.

After passing by one such swath, I could just barely make
out a low, wet meadow behind the blueberry. These mead-
ows are favored by some of our rarest plants, and to have
passed it by would have been a dereliction of duty. I wres-
tled my way through the sinuous blueberry trunks into the
small meadow. On the opposite side of the meadow was an
open pathway leading down from what turned out to be a
house hidden from sight.

Advancing rapidly down the pathway was the house
owner, a man I judged to be in his midfifties. "Six months
and a $1,000 fine," said the look on his face. I didn't even
complete the first sentence of my pond shore sales pitch
before he clutched me firmly by the upper arm and led me
firmly toward the pathway.

"This is private property," he said. Protesting with my
legal rights only would have meant more trouble.

Then a strange thing happened. Somewhat embarrassed,
I was looking down at the ground—at the meadow—during
my forced eviction, and noticed that the root of my trouble,
a rare plant, was growing there. A tiny, smug smile worked
its way out, and I was then and there reminded of a scene
from the movie *Rear Window.*

Grace Kelly has just been arrested for sneaking into the
apartment of suspected wife-disposer Raymond Burr. (Grace
is a trespasser, too.) Her mission had been to find the wedding ring of the missing wife to prove that the latter was
not away on a trip, but dead. The scene shifts to the cross-
courtyard apartment of her cohort, James Stewart, who is
watching the arrest through his binoculars.

He notices that Grace, her back to the window, is wildly
wiggling the fingers of her handcuffed hands. She is trying
to get Stewart's attention to show him that she is wearing
the tell-tale wedding ring.

My wedding ring was a thread-leaved sundew. Raymond
Burr had me by the arm for the moment, but I had the

goods on him and was headed straight for the plant police.

The plant police are nice people. They have to be, because Massachusetts has no law that requires private property owners to protect plants—rare or otherwise—on their land. I don't know how Mr. Burr responded to the news of my discovery, but I am confident that no trespasser picks his rare flowers.

CURSE OF THE ALEWIVES

IN THE EARLY 1980S, BRITISH NATURE DOCUMENTARIAN Sir David Attenborough and his crew were filming *The Living Planet*, which premiered in 1984. They came to Cape Cod, and I, a local naturalist, was asked to guide a camera crew to an alewife run. (An alewife is a kind of herring.) Adult alewives live in the sea but spawn in freshwater rivers and creeks.

We found a beautiful little spot where a small wooden bridge crossed narrow and shallow Pamet River in Truro. The small alewives were frequent but not abundant. Problem was, the camera crew determined the best shot would be if the alewives were swimming downstream, but none was heading in that direction. So the crew positioned me upstream just out of sight of the camera, from where I threw large sticks at the alewives—there are almost no rocks on Cape Cod—to make them turn around and swim toward the camera.

Now I find it incredible that I could have done such a thing, but at the time my guilty feelings were no more than a nuisance. It must have been the brush with fame that overruled my moral compass, and for that I was handsomely paid by karma: the entire event was left on the cutting room floor.

Disenchanted Isle

ABITATS HAVE SIGNATURES. CORDGRASSES SPEAK IN
unison of salt marshes. Water lilies tell of nutri-
ent-rich ponds. Beach grass writes of sand.
So what habitat might this be? "It is inhabited by
10,000 herring gulls, 1,000 brown rabbits, 400 to 500
bumblebees, 25 baby eider ducks, two scientists, and nine
juvenile delinquents."

This description, written by Jonathan Evan Maslow
and appearing in the March 1976 issue of *Country Journal*
(I'm a little behind in my reading), could only apply to
one spot on Earth: tiny Penikese Island at the end of the
Elizabeth Islands south of Falmouth on Cape Cod. The
number of individuals may have changed over the years,
but all the species mentioned in the clue are still present
except the delinquents, who left in 2011.

Penikese Island has never been settled in the sense of
a permanent community. But neither is it undisturbed. It
has been done over many times by a succession of human
activities. Let's call the island "unsettled."

Bartholomew Gosnold, who in 1602 set up a short-
lived sassafras mill at nearby Cuttyhunk Island, described
Penikese as a cedar-covered isle. We know that at the time
it was richly wooded with a variety of trees, including oak
and beech.

The first commercial use—no, let's rephrase that—the
first *legal* commercial use of the island was the harvesting
of its oaks for potash. This led to the second legal use: the

quarrying of the granite boulders left behind by the glacial ice sheet and exposed by the woodsman.

The very first commercial use? It is said the island's first entrepreneurs were piratic "moonspinners," who in the late 1600s from shore lured ships to unsafe waters at night by mimicking the lights of another boat.

Following the harvesting of oak, granite, and ships, there is little record of human activity until the late 1800s, but pasturage is inferred for the intervening time. More of that in a moment.

The modern history of Penikese Island began in 1873 when Louis Agassiz, the great naturalist from Harvard who decoded much of our glacial history, opened the nation's first summer natural history school there. Agassiz died soon after, and the school closed after its second session in 1874.

One of Agassiz's summer students, David Starr Jordan, conducted an inventory of the island's plants. Of the once-luxurious forests, Jordon wrote, "There is no trace left save the rotten roots of a solitary beech stump and a few branches of red cedar (Miller 2020)."

The island persists as a nearly treeless habitat, its forest seed bank having been exhausted. The most likely agent for that time-consuming work is sheep who, consuming over time, would nip every oak and beech sprout in the bud.

Following the collapse of the natural history school, Penikese reverted to the state of Massachusetts.

The next entry in our chronology is one of the island's darker periods. In 1905, it became a leper colony, one of only two in the United States. The other, better known, was in Louisiana. The quarantined were allowed to have their spouses live with them, but sex was forbidden, as it was believed the disease could be inherited. So there are only adults in the island's tiny overgrown cemetery.

The cemetery and remnants of stone walls are all that remain of the leper colony, plus a bad taste in the memory.

The colony closed in 1921, and the surviving inhabitants were shipped to Louisiana.

Maybe in recompense, or from fear of contamination, the island became a wildlife sanctuary a few years later, and it remains so today. Like Nomans Land, a wildlife sanctuary and bombing range off Martha's Vineyard, Penikese Island is at the leading edge of defining the limits of the land management concept known as multiple use.

In 1975, the state's Department of Youth Services set up the Penikese Island School to rehabilitate youthful offenders between ages fifteen and seventeen. The program, which closed in 2011, coexisted with wildlife management and scientific studies.

The natural history is just as bizarre as the human history—and related to it. An early task taken on by the fledgling sanctuary in the 1920s was the protection of what at the time was one of the state's most endangered birds, the herring gull. The program was an overwhelming success. (I joke, of course. Penikese had little to do with the current herring gull populations, other than being one more habitat overrun by them.)

Today's endangered bird is Leach's storm petrel, a seabird that nests on Penikese. The gulls have driven off the terns that used to nest on the island's beaches, but the storm petrel avoids the gulls by being nocturnal, and by its habit of nesting in the nooks and crannies of rock cliffs instead of on the beach.

So where does a petrel find rock cliffs on the sandy outwash deposits of Penikese? In the remnant stone walls of the leper colony.

Would that all our discarded shames be put to such good use.

Lulu Miller. *Why Fish Don't Exist.* New York: Simon & Schuster, 2020.

ALICE'S ROCK

A MONG THE BELONGINGS I CAN'T BEAR TO PART WITH is a small, smoothly rounded stone I found along a trail through the beech forest in Provincetown at the tip of Cape Cod. Stones often catch my eye, but this one caught a ride home. On it was a simple black line drawing that used the rock's shape to realize a very fat cat with a slightly annoyed look on its face.

On the back of the stone are the letters AMB, and I knew they were the initials of Alice M. Brock. A Provincetown artist, she was the title character in "Alice's Restaurant Massacree," a song composed in the 1960s by folk singer Arlo Guthrie, son of Woody. The song was inspired by true events arising from a 1965 Thanksgiving dinner in Stockbridge, Massachusetts. It has become something of a Thanksgiving tradition itself on New England radio stations and was the inspiration for Arthur Penn's film *Alice's Restaurant*, made in 1969 and starring Arlo.

Sometime around the early 1980s, Alice moved to Provincetown. Painting small stones became one of her expressions, and she set them free (for the taking) in the woods, at the beach, and in other delightful places. To look for one was the waste of a good walk.

One day a year Alice gave us a taste of what had inspired her folkloric fame, and it was faithful to the season. The Provincetown Art Association hosted an annual crafts fair around Thanksgiving. There was a food booth, and Alice did the cooking. It was another of those unassuming pieces of living history provided by quietly exceptional people, revealing the inner Provincetown to be a creative force and a celebration of life behind the glitter and crowds of its tacky exterior.

ANCIENT URGE

The pitch pines close around me,
small woods few bother to know
with their feet.
            from Marge Piercy, "Sand Roads"

D RY NEEDLES CRUNCH UNDERFOOT. BRITTLE OAK
leaves clatter like the scales of a mythic beast.
Only the occasional call of a bird enlivens the
dead of winter in the pine barrens of Cape Cod, a habitat
dominated by the low-growing pitch pine. There seems
almost nothing to recommend it. As a forest it appears
to be in disarray. As an individual tree it is asymmetrical,
unlike most other conifers. There is no obvious pattern in
the design of tree or forest. This Puritan-poor landscape is
not brochure worthy. It is not the Cape Cod of seagulls,
salt marshes, and endless sandy beaches.

Yet the pine barrens is the most common natural community on Cape Cod and is found in every town. It is pio-
neer and climax forest rolled into one, and without human
interference it can only be replaced by itself. Pollen grains
from core samples taken on the Outer Cape reveal that the
pine barrens has been a major component of the landscape
for seven thousand years. To a lesser extent the oaks are
participants in the barrens: scrub oak in more open areas,
black oak in older woodlands.

The barrens is quiet but not barren. In hollows, and
on slopes with their backs to the sea, there is protection

from wind-borne salt and sand, and a richer bit of soil
(though richer only by comparison). In these pockets of
habitat, the white oak, red maple, sassafras, and beech
are sometimes found. But the dry sand that is the bulk of
upland Cape Cod belongs to the pine.

Somehow, the pine feasts on that meager soil and in
so doing fills the Cape with life. This is the home of red
fox, great horned owl, and whitetail deer, of bobwhite and
ruffed grouse, of pink lady's slipper and spotted pipsissewa.

One creature stands out as the quintessential inhabitant
of the pine barrens. This is the whip-poor-will, a bird that
summers on the Cape and winters with the Floridians.
Year-round residency counts highly among Cape Codders,
but the whip-poor-will is so in tune with and dependent
on the attributes of the barrens that it can be forgiven for
its inability to survive the winter. It breeds there, and if
anything is more important than year-round residency to a
Cape Codder, it is to be born there.

The whip-poor-will spends half of its time—all in
daylight—on the ground, stone-still among the litter of
pine needles, scrub oak leaves, and twigs. Its feathers are
mottled browns and grays, its form nearly formless, a low
mound with a tiny beak and no neck. It is so sure of its
invisibility that it even nests on the ground, scooping out a
divot for, inevitably, two eggs.

The whip-poor-will feeds at night, especially at dusk
and dawn. Despite its tiny beak, it has a gaping mouth and
voraciously eats flying insects like mosquitoes and moths.
It is said that a whip-poor-will consumes more mosquitoes
in a single night than the touted purple martin eats in a
lifetime. (Oh, if only that were true.)

The Cape has not always been good habitat for this
helpful citizen. There were no whip-poor-wills in the
treeless plains of the nineteenth century. "The trees were,
if possible, rarer than the houses," wrote Thoreau about

Eastham, an observation that could have been applied to virtually any Cape town at some time during the past three hundred years.

Although it is the ancient urge of Cape Cod, the pine barrens of today is essentially an aftereffect of our having given up former land-clearing practices. Its future is even more precarious, as today's alterations offer no hope of restoration. The barrens desperately needs to be more than "small woods few bother to know with their feet."

Marge Piercy. "Sand Roads." *Atlantic Monthly* (August 1975).

JUST A CAT

UNTIL I MET TANSY, I DIDN'T THINK CATS WERE among the brighter lights in the animal kingdom. They seemed more instinctive than thoughtful. Cats spend a lot of time staring into space, as if their brains are in a holding pattern, waiting for some movement, sound, or smell to awaken a purpose. But I now have a great respect for the cat thinking process, and its awareness of how the world works. I thank Tansy for that. One evening I watched her perform a brave and wise act that revealed a conscious mind not unlike our own.

Tansy was part of a small troupe of feline gypsies herded by Irene, a biologist who lived in Provincetown at the tip of Cape Cod. At the conclusion of a successful courtship in the early 1980s, she moved into my small house on the edge of a Provincetown woods.

Irene arrived with three cats: Tansy, Winkin, and Mudlark. I was struck by their distinctive personalities. Winkin was aloof and could only be approached under her terms. Irene had found her as a kitten on a busy city street—so young she was still blind. Irene surmised Winkin's mother had given birth in the urban wild and dropped the kitten during a relocation of the litter. Irene became the replacement mom, and Winkin grew up thinking she was a human in a cat's body. Poor Winkin. She got along with no one.

Mudlark was skittish. The slightest movement or sound might send her into another room or under the bed. But she loved laps and petting, and her purring sounded like a motorboat coming down our drive.

The clowder soon expanded to five when Irene was flagged down by a part-Siamese cat. It happened in the beech forest that grows in the Provincetown dunes. Irene was bicycling through the forest when she was stopped by a sleek gray cat mewing along the side of the trail. Irene noticed that the small cat (soon to be named Minnie) was nursing and eventually found her litter beneath a fallen pine, an empty cardboard box nearby. Minnie was healthy looking and must have been a house cat. Apparently, she and her six infants had been boxed and rudely dumped in the woods. Irene fetched her animal transport cage and brought Minnie and her children to our home. All but one of the kittens were given away. The retainee, Buddy, acquired her name by a habit of crawling onto the forward part of one of Irene's shoes and staying there as Irene carefully walked around the house.

Tansy, the oldest and biggest cat, was the house warlord. It only took one whack to put another cat in its place forever—a whack accompanied by a look that said, "Do that again and I will have you for lunch, and you look pretty tasty." The rest of the time, Tansy was content to be the house diva, mellow and unassuming. You could pet her if you wanted, but she seldom asked for it.

Although I failed to notice it, Irene had observed that the house needed another mammal, a dog, in particular, a male English cocker spaniel named Cory. A purebred, Cory had been raised in a kennel. He grew up in a confined area whose width could be determined by measuring the diameter of the narrow circles he ran whenever he got excited. Even when he was out of doors with the whole world at his disposal, Cory ran in the same tight circles, confined by his imaginary cage. He always ran counterclockwise, which we attributed to the Coriolis effect, and that is how he got his name.

The Tansy Incident happened the evening Irene first brought Cory into the house. She set the transport cage down in the living room and opened its door. Cory stepped out, took one look at five wide-eyed cats, and hastily turned back into the cage, lying down on its floor, looking outward and alarmed. The five cats were spellbound. The moment seemed to last forever. I had no idea how it would resolve itself.

Tansy was sitting on the floor, facing the front of the cage from about eight feet away. She brought that forever moment to an end by standing up. Slowly, deliberately, Tansy walked toward the open door of the cage, toward the startled dog, who must have been at least three times her size. We were breathless. What on earth was Tansy doing? Cory, although obviously apprehensive, did not freak out as Tansy approached. He was lying against one side of the cage, with his body occupying about two-thirds of the cage floor. Tansy walked right up to the door, stepped into the one-third space remaining inside the cage, turned around, and lay down next to Cory.

It's impossible to say how long she stayed there, and it's important to note that Cory stayed there too. Even five seconds would have seemed an eternity, but I think it was closer to half a minute. Tansy then got up and walked out of the cage, ever so calmly. Moments later, Cory did the same, and the house was together.

It was one of the most extraordinary acts I had ever seen any nonhuman perform, establishing a new limit of credibility. Her behavior could only be explained by an awareness that the dog must be shown it was accepted by the cats, and possibly also to show the other cats that the dog could be lived with. She undoubtedly knew it could have ended badly, yet she had the courage to bring the olive branch anyway.

No doubt her wisdom came from age. A couple of years later, she began to fade, enduring a feline dementia.

Sometimes when we let her out, she would be gone too long. And once she never came back at all. Irene posted notices on neighborhood telephone poles, and about a week later we got a call from a woman who had a house on the harbor. There was a cat matching Tansy's description hanging out on the understructure of her pier. We found the cat on a cross beam below the pier's deck. She was facing the sea, the waves moving in and out beneath her.

As we approached, Tansy mewed in recognition. Had she forgotten how to get back home? Had she forgotten she had a home? Staring out to sea during the final stages seemed a human thing, something Winkin might do, the human trapped in a feline body. Tansy was just a cat, with a cat's practicality. I think she was there for the smell of fish.

SPELLBINDING MONOTONY

THERE ARE TWO MAIN FISHING WHARVES IN PROVINCE-
town, and they extend more than 1,000 feet out into
the harbor from the municipal parking lot. The distance
between them is about 400 feet. The parking lot bulkhead links
them, and together they form three sides of a rectangle open to
the sea.

One day two dolphins showed up between the wharves.
Whales and dolphins are common in waters off Cape Cod, but
rarely are these animals seen so close to shore in the town's
harbor. The dolphins were swimming side by side in a counterclockwise circle between the two wharves. On each circuit they
came close to the bulkhead along the edge of the parking lot.

The pace was slow, and periodically the dolphin on the
outside of the circle would begin to sink. The other then dove
down beneath it, and with its nose raised the sinking animal
back to the surface. Clearly the outside animal was sick or
wounded, and the other was keeping it from drowning. The
chosen location for this medical emergency suggested we and
our constructs posed less of a danger than their natural habitat.

Everyone in town made frequent visits to the harbor to
monitor the spellbinding monotony. This magnificent example
of nonhuman intelligence and compassion played out for
three days and nights, and then the dolphins were gone. We
all assumed it was a successful treatment and recovery.

Dead Phones for Dwayne

COURTESY OF A THANKSGIVING DINNER INVITATION, I briefly returned to Provincetown in November 2007; I had lived in the socially adventurous town for two decades beginning in the late 1960s. On the day before Thanksgiving, I took a reminiscent walk down Commercial Street, the aptly named strip of tourist shops edging the harbor. Back when fishing paid the bills, it was called Front Street. In summer, Commercial Street is a sluggish, suffocating river of flesh, but the rest of the year it is usually quite walkable.

On this day there were few other people, but one of them was Dwayne, a townie sitting alone on the bench in front of Town Hall, still talking to the voices in his head just as he did when I last saw him nearly twenty years before. His voice was raised and forceful, amply holding up his end of the conversation. Dwayne's mental condition was variously rumored to be the result of too many drugs or too little outcrossing. He still looked like a Chicago Seven radical, and his appearance and behavior could be quite alarming to anyone encountering him for the first time. But he had proven himself harmless over the years and was tolerated even by the authorities.

Just after I saw Dwayne on this most recent encounter, I was passed by a man who also was alone and talking. Coming toward me was another man, and he too was alone and talking. The difference between them and Dwayne (and I regard it as a small difference) is that the latter two men were talking on their cellphones.

And then it occurred to me: what Dwayne needs is a dead cellphone. Due to forgetfulness, he will need a boxful of dead cellphones, and a community committed to providing them. But with phone in hand, he will instantly look normal to tourists, who may think he is a latter-day Beat poet having an animated conversation with his publisher—or, more frequently, is on a conference call.

FROM THE FOUND JOURNAL OF
CAPTAIN MILES STANDISH

A literary reenactment of the Pilgrims' first day ashore in the New World, on what is now the Provincetown Peninsula at the end of Cape Cod. Captain Miles Standish has organized a reconnoiter, and among the party is young William Bradford, who will become leader of the Plymouth Colony.

. . .

AFTER THREE DAYS, HAVING REFRESHED OURSELVES upon the cold and deep harbor, seventeen of our number set out from the *Mayflower* to perceive the worth of this narrow parcel. As captain, I desired an adventure to cleave the rust from men and muskets. The woods thereabout were thick-grown and full of thorns, which gave us great relief to come upon sand hills, though to walk on sand is no great joy after a fair turn of the clock.

Presently we came to a huge inland sweep of the harbor at the end of which was a long marsh. All the while, we were upon the stretch of sand hills, and eagerly sought the firm high ground across the marsh for which our aching ankles were constructed. Some of our party, to save time, wanted to wade the marsh, but our clothes were already wet from wading ashore, and there were signs of affliction in a few noses. So I forced us farther upon the sand, and when we had finally circumvented the marsh to

higher ground, I thought: Here we are all the same, and
does it matter if we are an hour later in a course that is a
thousand leagues from yesterday, and knows not one foot
of tomorrow?

That evening we determined a low hill with good view
to sleep our first night on the coarse bosom of this wild
land. No adventure of any sort had fallen to us, but we set
out watches after I warned the men that an idle musket and
a mind gone home invite a knife to the throat.

I lay down, one eye upon the stars, the other upon the
watch, the better both to observe and protect my life. Lady
Sleep was slow to my bed but quick to leave. I awoke
before the first light of my first New World sunrise, having
suffocated the others in the bowels (an unpleasantly accu-
rate word) of our ship.

Our party brushed the web of night from its stiff
joints and set to breakfast: this a looseness of language,
for to call breakfast what we also eat at noon and supper
is more a nod to custom than to appetite. We chew—nay,
remill—hard-biscuits thrice daily with no other encouragement than a will to live and hunger's great tolerance. Two
months on the *Mayflower* of stale September and October
flour, and now November flour, is enough to set a man
against an army to gain half an acre of seed-wonting soil.

Nor is our water good, it being bitter upon the palate
after so much steeping of staves. Tillman, overthrown by
desire, cried out for "a cup of tea, or in the name of God
I'll be the Devil." And that sparked a fire to appease the
devil in us all. How unhappy our lot, that the Devil col-
lects the tolls on God's highway.

After tea I once again advised the men in the deport-
ment of their muskets, so that, though not knowing the
dangers of the place, we might at least not be a danger
to ourselves. Other than myself, there is hardly a soldier
among us. This is a great wonder to me and gnaws at the

edge of my sleep. For we have fled half a world—more, from one to another—without notion of conquest or compel of the unknown, with guessed-at charts, and only tales for experience. I fear it is our ignorance has got us here as much as our courage.

On our way to higher ground we found a spring welling with fresh water. Two months' deprivation was not only ended but nearly justified by the sudden pleasure. Even so, a few restrained themselves, afraid of a suspected vileness, as if the elements might differ here. But upon the hungry gulpings by most, the few fell to it.

Here we stopped for another round of hard-biscuits, and a better cup of tea. I sat and talked the while with Wm. Bradford. We have grown fond. His head is made of enough solid stuff to anchor our people to. William leads, not by force of will, but by example of his virtue. I am envious, but I am also joyed to see the subtle accumulation of power in one who does not seek it.

"You bring your journal even on this damp adventure," William said.

"It is my weaving," I replied. "It not only empties my head of its mundane businesses but fills it up again with play."

"How fare I in it, if at all I be there?"

"You fare well. That is, if you consent to be the fool to me as king."

"I'll be the fool, but to no king."

"If there is no king, the fool may lead."

"Then they are fools who follow."

"That is a proper government . . . ."

PART III.

STORIES FROM THE OUTPORTS OF NEWFOUNDLAND AND LABRADOR

These sketches are from travels in Newfoundland and Labrador that began in the summer of 1999. I was invited up from North Carolina by an old friend from Massachusetts. He had fallen so deeply in love with the eastern Canadian province that he bought a house there—not just any house, but the house at the end of the road, at the extreme north end of the Great Northern Peninsula, at the entrance to the Strait of Belle Isle. Labrador can be seen from his porch. The street in front is called The Tickle, and traffic is small fishing boats, whales, icebergs, seals, foxes, moose— and rarely, polar bears.

The anecdotes, encounters, and events were gathered during several visits, and the year is added when circumstances require. I am a botanist, retired since 2007, and in some ways this cobbled journey is like a botanical transect, long and linear sampling intended to pick up enough detail to get a satisfying glimpse of the habitat and its inhabitants. Nearly half of the population lives in small, isolated fishing villages called outports, and it is in rural and remote areas where traditions linger longest.

A Strange Thing from the Deep

A LIGHT DRIZZLE GREETED THE FERRY AS IT ARRIVED IN Port aux Basques, Newfoundland, six hours across Cabot Strait from Nova Scotia. A fog shrouded the low hills bordering the harbor, misty white hands trying to reclaim the land for a sea reluctant to give it up.

Later, I found a passage in John Gimlette's book *Theatre of Fish* with a similar image of Newfoundland from nineteenth-century American explorer Robert T. S. Lowell: "A monstrous mass of rock and gravel, almost without soil, like a strange thing from the bottom of the great deep, lifted up suddenly, into the sunshine and storm, but belonging to the watery darkness out of which it has been reared."

Newfoundland is nature's great experiment to saturate stone. The rocks seem always wet, even in the sun, which has no power to dry them. Bogs and fens are everywhere—in the valleys, on the moors, and up mountain slopes, where not even gravity can loosen the water.

But the rock is stubborn and not quickly washed away. It is the northern extent of the Appalachians, part of the oldest surviving mountain system on the planet, older than the Rockies, the Alps, and the Himalayas, formed on the ancient supercontinent of Pangaea.

After 480 million years of rain, snow, wind, freeze, thaw, and scouring glacial ice, the mountains have been worn to their nubs, but nubs that still reach half a mile high. The sea can only reclaim them one grain at a time.

John Gimlette. *Theatre of Fish.* New York: Knopf, 2005.

DORIAN AT THE DORYMAN
(OR, HOW A HURRICANE BLEW THE LID OFF HISTORY
AND REVEALED THE ORIGIN OF ACADIAN MUSIC)

DURING MY VISIT TO ATLANTIC CANADA IN 2011, I left a day early from my home in North Carolina to avoid an encounter with Hurricane Irene. But two days later the big blow-hard caught me anyway, in Cheticamp on Cape Breton Island, Nova Scotia. Friends were not surprised—they call me a hurricane magnet after so many encounters.

Eight years later, in September 2019, I again left a day early, to avoid Hurricane Dorian. As in 2011, I headed for Cheticamp, where—fool me twice, shame on me—Dorian was waiting. It was now called an extratropical storm, but its winds were still maxing at 90 mph, and 250,000 Nova Scotians lost power. (Let us not forget that more than 600 people lost their lives to this hurricane in the Bahamas.)

Dorian had virtually closed the old French town of Cheticamp. I arrived late afternoon, and the Doryman Bar was the only open establishment I could find. The wind was so strong I had to use my body as a lever against the door to gain entry. There were maybe fifteen patrons inside, and the view out the windows looked catastrophic.

But Acadian fiddler Chrissy Crowley was playing her heart out, bravely honoring a scheduled performance and uncertain about her twenty-mile drive back home. We were all on edge, because a power outage would bring a quick end to everything: fiddling, food, beer, and most important, comfort from the storm. Thankfully, the outage never came. These are the moments we keep.

The walls and windows of my cabin on the harbor thudded and wailed all night in the pounding wind and pelting rain. The experience was nearly identical to the noise and vibrations of stormy nights in a dune shack on the Provincelands of Cape Cod, and the revival of that memory put a shine on the bluster.

Next morning, the dozen old fishermen sitting in a Cheticamp café spoke a French that seemed as distant from Quebecois as Quebecois is from Parisian. Cheticamp is a lovely (though edgy) mixed bag: French fishermen, Celtic musicians, good restaurants, gorgeous natural setting, and often violent weather. It and its French bakeries sit at the beginning (or end, depending) of my favorite part of the Cabot Trail, the northwest coast of Cape Breton Highlands National Park.

Next evening I was in North Sydney waiting for the midnight ferry to Newfoundland. I had time to kill and did it mercifully in Tim Hortons, a Dunkin Donuts equivalent. Thanks to the serendipitous Doryman experience with Ms. Crowley, I decided to research what is called Acadian music (a form of Celtic music) and Acadia itself. Acadian music may be Cape Breton's proudest export and by far the one with the least environmental impact. It has a substantial presence on the island itself, with several album-producing musicians, and many venues where live music is played.

Here's a brief summary of what I found about Acadia and Acadian music:

Acadia (*L'Acadie*) was the first colony established in the part of North America known as New France, about 1604. By the early 1700s, New France included most of eastern North America west to the prairies and south to Louisiana.

The Acadian colony originally included all of the Maritime provinces: New Brunswick, Nova Scotia, and Prince Edward Island (P.E.I.), plus portions of eastern Quebec, Newfoundland, and Maine to the Kennebec River. Acadia was gradually overrun by the British, with Cape Breton and P.E.I. the last regions to fall, in 1763.

The Acadian diaspora, memorialized in Henry Wadsworth Longfellow's poem "Evangeline," happened mostly during the Seven Years' War (1756–1763) and was known as the Great Upheaval or *Le Grand Derangement*. The British deported about 80 percent of the French Acadians, most to what we now call the Thirteen Colonies. Many eventually made their way to Louisiana, where they became known as *Cajuns*, originally a pejorative term.

According to Wikipedia, some Acadians "who had been expelled from Nova Scotia and *Ile Royale* [New France name for Cape Breton Island] were permitted to settle in Cape Breton beginning in 1764, and established communities in northwestern Cape Breton, near Cheticamp, and southern Cape Breton, on and near Isle Madame."

In the 1800s, Scots began immigrating to Cape Breton in great numbers, primarily in response to what is known as the Highland Clearances, the removal or exodus of Highland clans due primarily to changes in agricultural systems from feudal to capitalist.

According to the Canadian Studies Center at the University of Washington:

> These Scottish settlers came to provide the dominant culture of Cape Breton, and the relative isolation of the island from the Scottish homeland meant that the Cape Breton traditions remained closer to their 19th century roots than their counterparts in Scotland.
>
> While Scottish music and dance [in Scotland] came under the wing of nationalist movements and

adopted a codified style for competitions, the music and dance of Cape Breton remained a community affair and kept the original dance rhythms and playing styles of pre–Clearances Scotland. Indeed, today Cape Breton musicians and dancers are sent back to Scotland to reeducate the Scots in their own traditional performance genres.

Well, how about that?

It appears that *Acadian* in the term *Acadian music* refers only to geography, as I have not found evidence of a French influence in the traditional Scottish music of Cape Breton. But the Acadian Scots and French are all descendants of refugees, and their cultures seem deeply intertwined.

Hilda Chiasson was Chrissy Crowley's keyboardist at the Doryman.

At Last, a Drinking and Dining Guide to the North Sydney Waterfront

NORTH SYDNEY, NOVA SCOTIA, IS WHERE I CATCH the six-hour ferry to Newfoundland and Labrador. The Cape Breton town is my Portsmouth, my Marseilles, the departure point to exotic lands. I spent some nights in that small town waiting for the ferry and came to know its understated, even retrogressive, charms. The old waterfront was drab and frequently in tune with its weather, befitting a town described as "nondescript" by a Canadian guidebook, which perhaps allowed the author to take the day off.

North Sydney's business district was pretty much confined to Commercial Street along the shore near the ferry terminal. The fronts of clothing and hardware stores, of restaurants and lounges were as plain and undemonstrative as the warehouses that shared the street. This was a commerce that depended on no outside callers, the buildings designed for function alone.

Like waterfront roads in other towns, Commercial Street is not straight but waddles to the left and right. This is a relic of the street having been built along the contours of the shore before the waterside was filled with the stores, warehouses, wharves, and docks of today. The street has become the old shoreline's fossil.

In late August 2009, the Commercial Street entrance to the Main Street Lounge (now defunct) had all of the glamour and none of the pretensions of an unlit back alley. A claustrophobic, plywood-framed dark hallway led to a staircase of similar temperament. The steps ascended into a space that, if not cheery, at least was softly lit and woody. It was about five in the afternoon, and two male patrons leaned against a bar tendered by Irene. My two drinking companions worked for Marine Atlantic ferry, North Sydney's biggest employer, and my transport to Newfoundland and Labrador. The ferry terminal was within easy walking distance of the lounge, at least for a sober person.

The primary topic at the bar was Marine Atlantic's newest ferry, put into service in April 2009. Opinion of the vessel was low that afternoon and, as I would soon learn, had been in descent even before its arrival in the Western Hemisphere in late 2008.

"It's from Russia, and it's caught fire twice and been disabled once at sea already," said Irene. "Nobody is surprised. If something works, it's not in Cape Breton."

During the new ferry's December 2008 crossing from its previous home port in Finland, the front loading ramp broke off. Shortly after it arrived in St. John's, Newfoundland, a fire broke out in one of two heating units. In July, a fire broke out in the other heating unit. It was briefly taken out of service in August after striking the landing dock in Port aux Basques, destination of the North Sydney ferry. And in October, it was disabled by a bomb threat, again in Port aux Basques. These human contributions to the downward spiral of its reputation were superfluous.

I abandoned my drinking companions for supper at Robena's (also now defunct), just down the street from the lounge. Like the adjacent businesses, Robena's exterior was so modest that I actually walked right past it, even though I was looking for it and had been there a few years before. The interior was simple with a high ceiling and old-fashioned booths. It was also a bakery, which filled the air with ovenly odors.

The seafood chowder I had at Robena's that evening
remains the best I have ever eaten, and I've eaten enough
to put an end to some anadromous run. It was a substantial chowder, the solids far outbulking the broth—so much
so that it arrived mounded in the center. Remarkably, the
center remained elevated above the suburbs and border
regions due to the density of matter throughout. And fish-
ness outweighed everything else combined, an ecumenical
school of haddock, herring, salmon, shrimp, crab, and scallops, plus chunks of potatoes and onions. The broth was
thick, rich, and creamy, no doubt from too much butter, if
there can be such a thing.

The waitress offered me a choice of tea biscuit, dinner
roll, or soda crackers to go with the chowder. I took my
chance with the tea biscuit, not knowing what it was. It
turned out to be like an American country biscuit, only a
little lighter and sweeter, and baked on the premises. Buttered and then soaked one bite at a time in the broth, the
tea biscuit nearly doubled the pleasure.

When I left the restaurant, I can't say the old waterfront's drabness had been dispelled, but an inner glow
rendered it of no account.

I returned to the Main Street Lounge after dinner at
Robena's. The earlier patrons had been replaced by two
more male ferry employees, one retired. The hapless new
ferry topic had weighed anchor, and conversation was now
about sports. The two men were seated at a table near the
bar. The younger man, about forty, was leaning back in his
wooden chair against the wall. He was the more serious of
the two, thoughtful and measured, his opinions schooled.
The subject turned to the unrequited love of hopeless
teams.

"For years my albatross was the Red Sox," I offered.
As soon as I said "Red Sox," the right arm of the

thoughtful man shot straight up—not willfully but as though it had been hoisted by a crane, the limp arm wrenched up and held erect against the wall. It was a spontaneous body language admission that he had spent years as a fan of the Boston baseball team and had paid a deep price for it. The look on his face was that of a man exhausted by pain.

Although the Red Sox had won two World Series within the five years preceding this barroom commiseration, there had been only dashed hopes for eighty-six years before that. No!—not dashed—hopes that had been toyed with, then shot in the gut, stepped on, and squished. Those wounds may have been healed by the recent victories, but the scars would never go away. After eighty-six years of defeat, even God was at risk.

Too Loud To Be Forlorn

ROSE BLANCHE IS A FISHING VILLAGE ON THE ISLAND of Newfoundland in eastern Canada. Its rocky setting and colorful houses attract artists and photographers. But it had a fault during my visit. A foghorn wailed for five seconds once a minute, twenty-four hours a day, every day. String all the blarings in one day together and they would last two hours.

The horn was too loud to be forlorn and blasted through every thought and conversation. While taking photos from a Rose Blanche wharf, I met a former resident who still had family there. The foghorn intruded upon our conversation.

"Did you ever get used to it?" I asked.

"Most of the time, yes," he said. "It used to blast only when it was foggy, but one day someone sabotaged the sensor, and now it's set to blast all the time."

Who would sabotage a foghorn sensor, and why? I thought it must have been someone impelled by a great anger, intent on leaving, never to return. It might inspire a novel, but one that would have to be written elsewhere.

THE CODROY COBBLESTONES

NEAR THE WHARF IN THE SOUTHWESTERN Newfoundland outport of Codroy is a small beach where the ocean stores cobblestones. They look like huge gray potatoes, their surfaces, angles, and corners smoothed and rounded by the constant rolling. One can hear a thousand disunited voices saying "cobble" as each wave rolls them twice, once coming in and again going out. One can also hear a thousand wooden shoes walking in a tunnel walled with stone, or a ruptured storage bin in a bowling ball factory, or a thousand skulls rolling down a bedrock slope in a catacomb.

Initially, I thought the cobble sound obeyed two pulses, the faster pulse with the waves, and a slower one with the tides. On a return visit I was greeted with silence at the cobblestone beach and assumed I would have to wait for high tide to hear the knockabout rocks again. So I interrupted three fishermen working with gear on the Codroy wharf to find out when the next high tide would be.

"Looks high now," one of them said, his tone indicating the conversation had run its course.

But I was not deterred. "When I was here last year, the tide was rolling the cobblestones on the beach below the road going up the hill over there." As I pointed toward the road, I realized I was on the verge of profound silliness but could not stop myself. "It was a wonderful sound, and I was hoping to hear it again. I thought it happened at high tide."

"Those was probably storm waves rolling the rocks," said another fisherman, the look on his face suggesting he was working hard at sounding normal for someone who wasn't.

THE UGLY STICK

THE OUTPORT MUSEUM AND TEA ROOM IN LA SCIE, Newfoundland, is owned by Valerie and Larry Whalen. Both are musicians and members of a local folk band, Codskiff, with Larry on guitar and banjo, and Valerie on drums, bodhran, spoons—and that most Newfoundlandic of instruments, the ugly stick. This homely noisemaker resembles (and often is) a broom handle. It is arrayed with bottle caps that jiggle together when the stick is pounded on the floor. The floor end of Valerie's stick was muted with a stuffed sock. This very cost-friendly instrument—made entirely of things found in every home—is a combination bass drum and castanets.

As I dined one evening in the tea room, two other men were present, both artists from Prince Edward Island. After a supper of stuffed cabbage and chocolate cake, we gathered in an adjacent room in the museum. Larry got out his guitar and Valerie grabbed her percussives. She also pulled out a sheaf of lyrics of folk songs from Newfoundland and the British Isles. The two men, members of a choir, happily joined in.

"Richard," scolded Valerie, "you must sing, too."

"I am best suited to be the audience," I said.

"Come on," countered Valerie, "everyone can sing."

"Not me," I protested. "I don't so much carry a tune as drag it along on the ground behind me."

Eclectic folk guitarist Leo Kottke described his voice as sounding "like geese farts on a foggy day." But that did not keep him from singing, nor was my metaphor of any use to me as Valerie stuffed lyrics into my hands.

FLUFFING DARK TICKLE

A BOTANIST BY TRADE, I WAS ORIGINALLY INTERESTED in learning the flora of Newfoundland, but over time I became acquainted with the people who live in the numerous little fishing villages called outports. Now I spend almost all of my time on the island visiting friends and making new ones.

Lounges (bars) are important to outport social life, so I have added them to my getting-to-know-the-locals curriculum. It is in the lounge that the Canadian sense of humor, of both men and women, is at its ribald best. Only problem is, at least in Newfoundland, lounges don't get busy until after 10 p.m. That's my bedtime. Age seventy is in my rearview mirror. One of the things you learn as you age is the inverse drinking rule: the older the hour, the younger you have to be.

It was only eight, on a late summer's eve at the Royal Canadian Legion lounge in Dark Tickle, a beautiful little outport. Just me and the barkeeper, Sophie. Most of the locals wouldn't show up for another couple of hours. Sophie looked to be in her midforties, but I later learned that her true age, about a decade older, had been obscured by a youthful outlook and black hair dye. More than once she told me whatever is said in the lounge she keeps in the lounge. Unfortunately for her, that restriction doesn't apply to me.

Reserved at first, Sophie soon gave me a tutorial on the varieties and progression of behavioral changes brought on by alcohol consumption. The bartender must not only know who will become what, but how that changing personality might interact with an evening's other volatile ingredients. She told me she never drank herself, except on Mummers Night, December 26, when she and friends dressed in disguise and went house to house to drink liquor and smoke cigars.

Around nine, a family from British Columbia entered the lounge: mom, dad, daughter, and son-in-law. The tall and handsome son-in-law was a search-and-rescue pilot for an arm of the Canadian military. His pretty wife was a Royal Canadian mounted policewoman, though if you ever brought up the joke imbedded in her job title, she could and probably would break you in half. Both were talkative and outgoing. Mom and dad, though not quite as forward, were also easy conversationalists. The parents were retired professionals, he a hydrologist, she a college administrator. The family quickly overwhelmed Sophie and me, and the evening took off in an unexpected direction.

The pilot and policewoman had just been transferred to St. John's, and the family was in Newfoundland for the first time. They bought me beers faster than I could drink them as we sped down the fast lane to alcohol's slurring of normality. Recorded music was playing, and the son and daughter decided to dance, pulling mom and dad onto the dance floor with them.

(Typical of Newfoundland lounges, the great majority of the legion's space is devoted to dancing. From what I have seen, Newfoundland is the proof of British playwright George Bernard Shaw's observation that dancing "is the vertical expression of a horizontal notion.")

Then the daughter pulled me off my stool—somewhat forcibly, as I am less a dancing fool than a fool while dancing. Her husband had already pulled Sophie out from behind the counter. Mercifully, the dance party broke up after the first song. The family wanted to be "Screeched in."

Sophie refused, bless her traditional heart. "It is an official ceremony, and we are lacking important ingredients," she said, somewhat inflating the actual level at which the hazing-like ceremony is conducted. Traditional Screech-ins are commonly held in lounges and make honorary Newfies of mainlanders. Typically, the ceremony involves participation in a silly skit, kissing a dead cod on the lips, eating something most foul (though quite tasty to them), and chugging a jigger of Screech, Newfoundland's rum. (As rums go, it is better chugged than sipped.) A Screech-in will determine whether you, like them and the Japanese, are willing to put almost anything in your mouth.

Sophie nonetheless did bring out a bottle of Screech and poured us each a jigger.

"I'm going swimming," the son then said enthusiastically. To me, that made him insane as well as drunk. Just the thought of Newfoundland's hyperborean waters gives me goose bumps.

There was a deck aside the legion hall, with steps leading to a dock. He said it would be the fourth time he had gone swimming in the bay that day, and we learned from his wife that the first three times he was naked. She rushed out after him with her camera.

When he returned from the swim, I surmised it must have been unbearably cold. But he said no, it wasn't cold until he got out of the water. He dried off in his clothes. His wife returned with several digital photos, which she gleefully shared with the rest of us, including her mom and dad. The photos provided indisputable proof, fore 'n' aft, that her husband had swum naked. I had never met a family like this before.

The effect of cold water on the human body entered the conversation, and our search-and-rescue pilot began to gesticulate charade-like near his groin. He kept mumbling something about "fluffing." Sophie and I were dumb-founded by where this seemed to be going. His wife, in a loud tone used for addressing complete idiots, said "Penis!" Fluffing, apparently, had something to do with her husband's penis. Though Sophie and I still didn't know exactly what he meant, *fluffing* quickly became the word of the evening.

(When I got to a friend's house the next day, we searched Google and discovered *fluffing* is a term in the porn industry. A *fluffer* is a stagehand who either orally or manually prepares the male porn star for his stand-up routine. *Fluffing* was elevated to word of the month.)

Meanwhile, back in the Dark Tickle lounge, our pilot had landed behind the counter, where Sophie said, "You're not supposed to be back here." To this he replied in his resolute yet well-mannered drunkenness, "I want you to go stand behind them"—pointing to me and his father-in-law—"so I can take a picture of all of you." Sophie complied, coming out from behind the bar and reaching her arms around our backs. But instead of her hand going for my shoulder, she slid it under my arm, and her fingers deftly found one of my nipples, which she began tweak-ing—or fluffing, as the effect is similar, though differing of course by a few magnitudes of degree on the pleasure scale.

The more I get to know these people, the stranger they become. All of my prior concepts of the Canadian charac-ter have been tossed overboard.

Two weeks later, on returning to Dark Tickle from Labrador, I learned that the swimming incident had been witnessed by town folk out for an evening stroll by the harbor. The search-and-rescue pilot had become known as the Dark Tickle Streaker. Sophie had a hard time convincing the locals that our pilot had not flown naked in the lounge.

The legion lounge was crowded during this second visit, even though it was only six in the evening. There had been a funeral that afternoon for a well-known resident, and death has no equal for unstopping the taps. Most everyone there was already plastered, including a young fisherman from Port au Choix whose words slurred to such an extent that I don't think even he understood them.

At one point during these festive last rites, Sophie came up from behind and wrapped me in a hug that, though devoid of fluffery, conveyed unequivocal intimacy.

And now I think I have a clue as to the reason for all of this randy behavior. As summer wanes, the Canadian libido rises to the challenge of luring winter's cheapest heat source, a bedmate. Apparently, even seventy-year-old equipment will do.

WOULD YOU LIKE A PARABLE
WITH YOUR COFFEE?

THE WAITRESS BEHIND THE COUNTER AT THE GRANITE Coffee House in Woody Point, Newfoundland, had a soft punk aura with short hair that wanted to be but wasn't quite spiky. She looked like she ought to be wearing safety pins or other skin-piercing metal. Although her face was appealing, it had a worried or even hardened look, as if she were restraining an anger.

I had to listen very carefully to understand her strong accent. Every outport has its own, often with a unique vocabulary to go with it. Sometimes I leaned in and asked her to repeat something as if I were hard of hearing. Once I even cupped my ear. I have this notion that she or anyone else with a hard-to-understand outport accent might feel put down by our failure to communicate, that it might be interpreted as part of that unreasonable sense of cultural superiority and inferiority that exists between urban and rural areas.

I was unsuccessful in my attempts to get her to smile, and she didn't volunteer any conversation after answering a question. During one of her breaks, I mentioned that a folk music concert was happening in the local theater that evening.

"That's not my kind of music," she said.

When I told her it was about the history of the Basques in Labrador, she looked annoyed, did not reply, and turned

to speak to the two women she was sitting with. I felt
shunned, that my interests were of no interest to her, and
worst of all, that maybe she didn't like me. This is a crushing blow to someone who works hard at being liked—in
this case, apparently too hard.

When I came to the coffeehouse the next morning,
much to my surprise she asked if I had enjoyed the concert. She spoke with an easy, unaffected enthusiasm, and
for the first time I saw her smile. In an instant she healed
all of my self-inflicted wounds. Her disinterest the day
before had nothing to do with me. She had given me a
low-cost lesson in how vulnerable my self-esteem is to the
views of others.

Fisherman's Brewis—Almost Edible

FISHERMAN'S BREWIS (PRONOUNCED "BREWS") IS AN anachronism from the earliest stages of development of fish and clam chowders, when hardtack ("sea biscuits") were a central ingredient. Brewis is what happens to hardtack when it is soaked in water overnight. Hardtack is a durable cracker that was a major source of limited nutrition on nineteenth-century ships, and during the U.S. Civil War. It often consists solely of flour after the water is baked out of it, and if kept dry can last for years. There is a joke among Civil War reenactors that hardtack made during the 1860s tastes just as good now as it did then.

In Newfoundland, fisherman's brewis was once the main meal for fishermen on a boat and often a breakfast on shore. It is still eaten today and is on the menu of some outport restaurants.

To make fisherman's brewis, the soaked hardtack is boiled or fried with fresh or salt cod and pieces of fatback pork; the pork is called "scrunchions" when fried. These mostly white ingredients suggest a meal that might seem more a dare than a dinner.

Brewis does provide a direct sensory connection to the former meagerness of outport life. In his book *The Labrador Coast*, Canadian naturalist and geologist A. S. Packard described a meal he was served in a local home during his survey of southern Labrador in 1861:

> Accepting our hostess's kind invitation to take
> dinner, we sat down to a characteristic Labrador

midday meal of dough balls swimming in a deep
pot of grease with lumps of salt pork, without
even potatoes or any dessert; nor did there seem
to be any fresh fish. The staples are bread and salt
pork; the luxuries game and fish; the delicacies an
occasional mess of potatoes, brought down the St.
Lawrence once a year in Fortin's trading schooner.

Because of the challenge it presents, brewis has a role
in the right of passage for island visitors. If I were to recommend a place to eat fisherman's brewis—and I'm not—
it would be a restaurant in Port au Choix. Pronounced
"port-uh-SWAH," the town's name derives from *Portuchoa*,
a Basque word meaning "little harbor." (I am withholding
the name of the restaurant so this can't be construed as a
review, though a clever reader with unbridled taste should
have little trouble locating it.)

This restaurant serves some of the best traditional food
along the west coast of Newfoundland, and I have had ex-
cellent seafood dinners there. With enormous courage, the
restaurant serves what must be regarded as a gourmet (thus
oxymoronic) setting of fisherman's brewis, which it calls
Salt Cod with Brewis on the menu. I had wanted to try salt
cod after reading Mark Kurlansky's book *Cod: A Biography
of the Fish That Changed the World* and learning the important role the salt-dried fish had played in world history.

The partly rehydrated and desalted fish was somewhat
fleshy but much chewier than fresh cod. Even after soaking, the salt content remained high, but that turned out
to be a blessing considering in what manner the other
ingredients arrived. The brewis and boiled potatoes were
cooked separately without seasoning, not even salt, the
curse of the English. As Harvard botanist M. L. Fernald
observed during visits in the 1910s and '20s, "At most
places in Newfoundland we get the horrible English cooking, gone a few degrees worse."

The serving plate was large with enormous helpings of the salt cod, brewis, and potatoes, as if proof were needed that you can have too much of a bad thing. In the center of the plate was a small bowl filled with scrunchions and chopped onions floating in the pool of fat in which they had been fried. This "sauce"—I'm quoting the waitress here—could be poured on the all-white fish, brewis, and potatoes, or used as a dip. The scrunchions admittedly were tender and crispy, but for nutritional benefit one might as well have been chewing bullets.

The waitress told me that it is common for Newfoundlanders to sprinkle sugar on their brewis, and then eat it with the scrunchion sauce. I thought this was a preposterous idea but tried it anyway. The sugar turned out to be something of an improvement, though that should not be taken as an endorsement, as almost anything would have been. The meal mercifully ended with a traditional dessert of lassie (molasses) bread and tea.

Those who ignore my warning should plan on waiting five days before eating again, to allow the body time to unplug itself.

Mark Kurlansky. *Cod: A Biography of the Fish That Changed the World.*
New York: Penguin, 1997.

A. S. Packard. *The Labrador Coast.*
Charleston, S.C.: Nabu Press, 2010 [1891]. Reproduction.

GHOST IN THE ATTIC

DURING A VISIT TO CONCHE, AN OUTPORT ON THE Great Northern Peninsula, I met a man working on his house.

"Some people say it's haunted by the ghost of a woman," he told me. "She's been seen in the attic, and I've heard strange noises coming from there. One man saw her in the early morning running from the house to the shore in a nightgown.

"The story goes that back in the 1700s a fellow left Ireland for Newfoundland, leaving the woman behind. Somehow her ghost made it here.

"My grandfather lived in the house, and he used to row out to the Gray Islands with his fishing partner. People on shore said they could see three persons in the boat as it left the harbor.

"I'd like to see her. I'm hoping she's a blond."

I Eat a Sea Mammal

E VERY SUMMER I SPEND AT LEAST A WEEK IN RED BAY,
Labrador, on the Strait of Belle Isle. It is the location
of a sixteenth-century Basque whaling and fishing
center and in 2013 was designated as a UNESCO World
Heritage Site. I always stay in the same lodging, the second
floor of a former fish stores. In its original use, fishermen
would have gathered there in winter to mend their nets,
warmed by a woodstove and, I like to think, by a sip or
three of Screech, Newfoundland's rum.

The lodging has a small but well-appointed kitchen. I
eat my morning and noon meals there. Over the years I
have grown closer to the lodging's owners and eat supper
in their small restaurant. It allows me to pursue one of my
favorite hobbies, the browsing of traditional regional foods.

But I had not fully considered the impact location
would have on the traditional menu. I was in the ecotone
between the outport societies of Newfoundland and southern Labrador, and the more isolated and trapper-descended
people of Labrador north of the Strait of Belle Isle.

Red Bay is at the southern edge of a culture that had
been created by and for the Hudson's Bay Company in
the early 1800s. The company had been the primary if not
exclusive European presence in Labrador, with a monopoly
on the fur trade. Many of its trappers, maybe a majority,
were recruited from the Orkney Islands in Scotland, and the
immigrant Scots married local Innu and Inuit women. (The
Innu are related to the Cree.) Today these melded blood

lines are well-represented in Labrador. Hunting remains an intimate part of Labrador life, even more so than on the island of Newfoundland. My education in the indigenous edible fauna was about to take a new turn.

I had spent a short time in Red Bay in 2007 with two friends from Cape Cod. Our visit coincided with the capelin run, and we asked our hostess Marilyn if the small fish were eaten in any form other than the rubbery dried version some fishermen keep in their pockets to eat as a snack.

(Imagine Miss Manners writing for outporters: "For best dining results, be sure to brush the lint off your pocket fish, and add, oh, maybe two gallons of air freshener to each load of laundry.")

Marilyn said the capelin were great breaded and fried. After we finished lunch and left the restaurant, she called her uncle and asked him to bring her some he had caught that day. At supper she surprised us with a plateful of breaded and fried capelin as an on-the-house treat. They were crisp, tender, and delicious—and cooked with all the organs their parents had given them. Capelin are related to smelt and are a favorite food of humpback and minke whales.

During a chat with Marilyn in 2009 about traditional indigenous foods, she said, "I have something I want you to try." As she headed to the storage area at the back of the restaurant, I braced myself, because Marilyn is descended from Inuit, Innu, and Scottish lines. She returned with a jar of very dark meat. It was from an adult seal her family had killed the previous spring. The meat had been preserved by packing it in Mason jars, then placing the sealed jars in a pot of boiling water. (The pun could have been avoided, but why?)

The offer triggered a three-part conflict. Accepting it was contrary to the default setting of my environmental ethic but would be the proper social response. The third part was my mission to sample traditional foods. Be careful what you wish for and know your latitude.

"I'll bring you a helping with your supper," Marilyn said. My internal conflict left me speechless, and my silence was assent by omission. I was a coward to my environmental ethic, but a hero to my adventurous palate. That evening supper came with a side plate of seal rib meat. I thought it might have a fishy flavor, being of the sea, but instead it had the flavor of organ meat, as if it had been cooked with liver. My gag reflex lurked in the background but never came into play.

There's nothing like a good helping of seal ribs to bring unresolved meat-eating issues to a head. I gave much thought to carnivores, omnivores, and herbivores, to wild and domestic, native and immigrant, subsistence and commercial—and to our animal kingdom hierarchies, where our opinions and arguments are almost always anthropocentric. The more an animal behaves like us, the less likely we are to want to kill it. How odd for a species so ready to kill its own.

After careful consideration (and rationalization), I realized there is a clause in my environmental ethic that permits me to eat seal at Marilyn's table, but not at my own. My "permission" doesn't come from the fact that seal eating by Labradorians is a cultural tradition. Traditions are not self-justifying and must be measured by their impacts and relevance in the present, and by their predictable consequences. I judged, hopefully correctly, that the species in question could withstand this smaller impact as long as the larger impact is prevented. No one—not Inuit, not Innu, not Scot—can legally hunt and eat the endangered North Atlantic right whale.

The authority for my seal-eating exemption was granted by Buddha, who (with a bow to Miss Manners) said, "Eat what is put into your bowl." That's my cover for now. The Labradorians are on their own.

(Newfoundlanders and Labradorians are the people clubbing baby seals in those hideous videos we and British royalty watched with horror years ago. Although the killings in the videos were not a necessity, they were the remnants of something that once was. What the videos didn't tell us was that northern Newfoundland might not have been settled by Europeans before the twentieth century without the seal harvest in the spring, as the Native Americans had done before them. Now the harvest of baby seals is no more necessary than the harvest of calves, lambs, kids, and suckling pigs. You wouldn't want to see those videos either.)

During my visits, Marilyn's family invited me to their traditional Sunday dinner, known throughout Labrador and Newfoundland as a Jiggs dinner. *Jiggs* is generally believed to have come from the name of a character in the *Bringing Up Father* comic strip who loved corn beef and cabbage. But Jigg is also the nickname for a fisherman, derived from a method of line fishing, and it too may lay claim to the origin of the dinner's name.

A Jiggs dinner is similar to a New England boiled dinner, featuring salt (corned) beef boiled with cabbage, potatoes, turnips, and carrots. Unlike in New England, however, it is served without horseradish. One year I brought up a bottle of horseradish sauce but couldn't convince anyone to try it. "It will make a great joke on someone," Marilyn said laughing, and I could see in her look that she was scrolling through a list of potential victims.

I have had Jiggs dinners elsewhere in the province, and

typically the helping of salt beef has been small, very salty, and tough. The salt of course is what historically protected it from spoiling. The toughness I thought might be due to the quality of meat available for curing. The last bite could be chewed all afternoon if one so desired.

The Jiggs dinners with Marilyn's family were major social events. Parents and siblings had driven that morning from their homes up north, a distance of more than a hundred miles on the dusty, rocky, and potholey Cartwright road (since paved). And they would return home that evening.

Marilyn, the primary chef of her restaurant, did not let her skill go to waste at the Sunday dinner. In addition to the traditional salt beef, roots, and tubers, she provided an ample amount of tender and moist roast chicken. Indigenous fauna also appeared, including seal, the dark-breasted eider duck, a gamey-flavored ptarmigan from western Labrador called "partridge," and char from a river to the north, looking and tasting like its kin, salmon. Marilyn once apologized for the absence of porcupine, a popular meat north of the strait. But no apology was necessary from where I sat. I remain reluctant to try rodent, even if it does come with its own toothpicks. Maybe all it will need is a little horseradish.

Marilyn's Jiggs dinner typically ended with partridge-berry pie warm from the oven, giving a soul-puckering finish to a memorable feast. The invitations were an honor, a welcoming not just to dinner but to the family, and to Labrador.

GUTTING TURBITS

"YOU MIGHT WANT TO GET DOWN TO THE WHARF,"
Marilyn said as I emerged from my lodging in Red
Bay one morning. "The boats are riding low in the
water; they're full of herring."

From my room on the second floor of the former
stores, I had seen a few of the small open boats come
into the harbor, each with one fisherman. Powered by an
outboard engine, they weren't much bigger than rowboats
and had no cabins, just enough room for a man and
his maximum catch. Water was lapping at the gunwales.
One more fish and the boat might have sunk beneath the
smooth surface of the bay.

Down at the wharf, a small crew was helping to un-
load the fish. I struck up a conversation with two women
who were part of the crew and would be processing the
herring at the fish plant in L'Anse au Loup that evening,
twenty-five miles down the winding road. They were
second-shift union workers, and the shifts were a matter
of seniority. Senior workers got the first shift and worked
during the day. The second shift not only worked at night
but had to clean up the processing area when work was
done. And if the catch was small, there might only have
been enough work for the first shift.

Those were the two rungs on their career ladder, and
the rungs were many feet apart. One of the women had
been doing time on the second shift for twelve years, the

other for twenty. The fish plant, and fishing itself, were
almost the only jobs around. It had been that way for a
long time, but now there were fewer fish.

"You're the rookie," I said to the woman with twelve
years on the second shift. She said the herring work bored
her. "It's too routine, no variety. It's a lot more fun working with turbits. They have to be gutted." I successfully
maintained a stoic expression in response to this measure
of how different our lives were.

"We just work the season, May to September, and get
the winter off," she continued. (And winter really does
stretch from October to April.) Typically, the fish-plant
season began with cod, followed by "turbit" (turbot, a
flounder) and capelin (a small smelt), then finished with
herring. The outporters may have had the winter off—
financed by what everyone called "E.I.," employment
insurance—but it was hardly an idle time, what with wood
gathering, subsistence hunting, repair of houses and fishing
gear, and trips to the cabin. Almost everyone seemed to
have a winter cabin reachable by skidoo (snowmobile).
There may not have been any money to be made in
winter, but just about the worst (and most inappropriate)
thing you could call an outporter was lazy.

I learned from the twenty-year veteran of the second
shift that the fish-plant rookie was the mother of Shery
Lynn Butt, Miss Newfoundland and Labrador in the
2003–2004 contest to determine Canada's entrant in the
Miss Universe pageant. I had known for a few years that
the beautiful Shery Lynn was from Red Bay. But it was a
bit of a surprise to learn that her mom was the fisherwom-
an at the wharf helping with the unloading of the herring
she would process that night. Mrs. Butt was plain-looking,
her bearing suggesting a practical woman whose ambitions
were already being met or were only one shift away.

The contrast between mother and daughter reflected

the rapidity of change taking place in southern Labrador. The daughter had leapt into the modern world, experiencing a sea change. But her mom's sea had hardly changed at all, except for fewer cod. At the time of my visit, Shery Lynn was still aspiring to be the most beautiful woman in the universe, which for all I know is more work and less fun than gutting turbits.

A Bear Ponders My Edibility

ONE DAY IN SEPTEMBER 2009, WHILE EXPLORING A broad ridge top called The Battery in southern Labrador, I found an intriguing habitat: isolated ponds in sandy and rocky soils where water levels went up and down with the groundwater. A botanist by trade, I was familiar with these habitats from Cape Cod to Florida. They are noted for their biological diversity and rare species, many of which are only seen when water levels are low.

Water levels were low on The Battery that September, and I was able to conduct a reasonable inventory of plant species at the first pond I saw. But much to my surprise and chagrin—even, perhaps, a modicum of terror—a black bear suddenly appeared on the shore of the second pond, rudely in the middle of my inventory. After an awkward assessment of intentions, or "interview," as John Muir called his black bear encounter, the bear escorted me out, even though I was there first.

For almost twenty years I made a living conducting natural habitat surveys in North Carolina. During that time I had been confronted by a number of animated assailants, but never a bear. I had been captured by marines on Camp Lejeune, eyed by swimming alligators too stupid to know how easy it is to overturn a pokeboat, and attacked during seaside surveys by terns that employed both fore and aft gunneries—that is, jabbed my head with their beaks and despoiled my head with butt filth. I have been stopped short by a hissing, floating, gape-mouthed water moccasin while wading hip-deep in a pond. Until the Labrador bear, that was my most terrifying moment, as the body part most readily available for a water moccasin strike was my belly. I have been driven from habitat by sky-darkening mosquitoes and airborne piranhas called deer flies. And I have been nibbled to distraction by chiggers and ticks. All are toothsome or beaksome aggressors who can penetrate the skin with oral parts, though the marines less frequently attack in this manner.

Among these predators, only the marines and alligators were capable of killing me on the spot. I escaped the Marines the same way they found me, through a portal into a parallel universe. They were in training for war and at rifle point ordered me to kneel on the savanna I had been surveying (for them), hands clasped behind my back. But because I was from a parallel universe, they could only pretend to capture, bind, and blindfold me.

The alligators, as I said, are too stupid to realize I was as easy to get as a clam in an open shell, and with a whole lot more calories. The pokeboat is a sort of kayak-canoe love child primarily used to fish quiet southern waters. I paddled the rivers and tidal creeks of southeastern North Carolina with the assurance of coworkers that gators do not attack things larger than themselves. The pokeboat was 11 feet long, but local gators are known to grow to 14 feet, meaning I did not have full coverage under the assurance policy. I most frequently saw them swimming with just their snout and eyes above water. Whatever their size, they continued on their way. But being eyeballed by a swimming gator is always scary.

Unarmed, I was mostly unprepared for the Labrador bear. I hadn't seen a bear of any breed in nearly twenty years, and never while walking alone in the wilderness. I knew there were black bears in Newfoundland and Labrador, but outdoors my thoughts had been of the polar bear,

the largest terrestrial carnivore on Earth. An adult polar
bear can weigh 1,500 pounds, and these behemoths occasionally showed up along the southern Labrador shore,
even along the north shore of Newfoundland, having
come south in spring to feed on newborn seals, and rarely
floating in on summer icebergs.

I wasn't thinking about bears at all, since I was a few
miles from the Atlantic shore, and several hundred feet
above it. (I thought I was out of polar bear habitat but
have since learned they will venture inland in that region.)
There is not much to commend stumbling on a black bear
in the wilderness, but the tone and outcome likely would
have been much different if it had been a polar bear. For
starters, I'd be writing my obituary here.

The first pond, where I successfully conducted my
plant inventory, is along Labrador Road 510. It is called
Funnel Pond, appropriate for its circular shoreline and
up-and-down movement of the water. The second pond,
which I now call Bear Pond, lies a little more than a half-
mile in from the highway. A dirt road passes by its southern end, and I parked on a slope above the shore. This
pond is linear, extending northward from where I parked
for about a quarter-mile and averaging about 200 feet
wide. As at Funnel Pond, water levels were low, exposing
a good half of the sandy and rocky pond basin below the
shrub-bordered high-water shoreline.

I began my plant inventory heading north along the
east shore, almost immediately seeing plants I hadn't seen
at Funnel Pond, a good start. After about fifteen minutes
and one-third of the way up the east shore, a beautiful
red fox suddenly appeared about 500 feet ahead of me.
It never saw me and trotted around the north end of the
pond, disappearing into the thicket on the slope above the
west shore. Five minutes later the bear appeared where the
fox had entered the east shore—my shore—only this time I

was about 300 feet away from the wild animal.

At first the bear didn't see me, and like the fox it headed toward the pond's nearby north end. But as it turned to the west, it saw me and stopped in its tracks. I was already stopped in mine. It is said bears don't see well, but I was standing still and maybe 400 feet away, and it never took its eyes off me.

I am not able to compare the feeling that comes from being in the gaze of a top-tier carnivore that is trying to figure out if I pose a threat to body or territory or am suitable for dinner. The bear was doing what a dozen gurus had failed to do: bring me to total and continuous focus in the present. The great majority of what I felt was fear, but there was also a bit of a thrill, a heightened awareness that this was a very special moment in my life, whatever the outcome.

As I assessed my vulnerability and marshaled my options, the bear just stood there, its body facing west, but its head turned south toward me. I slowly began to back up. But the pond's rocky shore made walking difficult in the direction I wasn't looking, so I turned around and continued in a more sure-footed manner. I frequently looked over my shoulder to see what Mr. Bruin was up to—I'm assuming a male since no cubs were present—and he continued to stand still and watch me. The bear then ambled—a lumbering amble, bony and muscular—up the west shore slope and into the thicket where the fox had gone, disappearing from view. I guessed he was following an animal trail, not the fox, though knowing full well the fox was not far ahead.

The consideration of options was easy, as there were so few of them. If he had charged, I would have thrown stones, the only weapon available. The exposed pond shore had every size of throwable stones in abundance. I mentally selected stone baseballs should the bear approach within 100 feet, and I would throw as many as quickly as I could, aiming for dead center. If those didn't stop it, I would hoist a heavier stone above my head and run at the bear yelling and, if necessary, do my best to give it a major league headache. I had thought about this should I ever be charged by a polar bear. This course of action seemed preferable to passively being chewed and clawed in a fetal position as recommended by some wilderness experts. And I would look as big as I could. Size is important to bears.

It is commonly believed that black bears without cubs are less likely to attack than brown bears (grizzlies) and polar bears, and I was counting on this bear to heed those beliefs. But in truth I didn't know what experts had recommended as the right action for an "interview" with a male black bear. Nor did I know the meaning of the various aspects of black bear behavior. I would be in for a surprise when I finally had a chance to do the research.

After the bear disappeared into the thicket above the west shore, I continued in a determined but less concerned manner toward the south end. My survey had been nullified, but as I neared the beginning of the trail that led up the open slope to my truck, I saw another plant species new to my list. As I knelt to collect it, my peripheral vision detected movement behind my shoulder, and I turned my head to see that the bear was no more than 150 feet behind me. He had come down the west side of the pond undetected and was now walking on the exposed shore. The moment I looked at him, he turned to the east and stopped, facing his head toward me as he had done during the first encounter. (So much for bears having poor eyesight.) I dropped the plant specimen, stood up, and began ascending the trail up the open slope—not running but ready to run. About halfway up I turned to look and was relieved to see he had not moved closer.

The bear's behavior suggested he was just curious, or

maybe territorial. But I couldn't let go of the notion that it might have been a diner's curiosity, wondering whether he could afford the price of "today's catch." He might have considered me too old and stringy to have been worth the effort. He no doubt also recognized me as the species that threw things at him as he tried to retrieve good-smelling objects from garbage cans. We may have been of similar minds, unsure whether to fight or flee.

John Gimlette, in his book *Theatre of Fish*, describes an encounter with a black bear at Nain in northern Labrador. It too seemed "undecided whether to run for it or eat me." Gimlette managed to slip away but took with him the "sensation of being edible."

The young Winston Churchill wrote in *The Story of the Malakand Field Force*, "Nothing in life is so exhilarating as to be shot at without result." My response was more euphoric relief than exhilaration, but I now know the realm of which he spoke.

Safely in my Tacoma, I headed toward the highway. But with a rationally challenged decision, I stopped at Funnel Pond where I had made the earlier inventory. I needed another specimen of a grass that had been difficult to identify. This pond was only a half-mile from Bear Pond, a distance Mr. Bruin could have covered in a minute when running with purpose. I was as wary as a burglar in a house of thieves.

After returning home from eastern Canada, I looked at a few websites devoted to bear encounters. There seems to be general agreement that it is a good thing to let a bear know you are a human by waving your arms and talking in a quiet, calm voice. (Frankly, those actions seem contradictory to me.) There is also general agreement that one should quietly back away while talking in that calm voice, apparently for as long as the bear is in view.

If the bear exhibits threatening behavior, the Center for Wildlife Information's site recommends yelling and throwing sticks or stones. But the weapon of choice if the bear closely approaches is pepper spray. The website of MountainNature says it should be used only as a last resort, when the bear is within 15 feet. Beyond that and the spray is likely to be too dispersed to be effective. The website also recommends that the pepper canister be immediately discarded, since the smell of pepper, contrary to spray in the eyes, is an attractant.

If a black bear physically attacks, some sites advise fighting back with whatever is available, even punching it in the eyes and nose, while others recommend assuming the fetal position and rolling with the bites and blows.

I was surprised to learn my bear may have been exhibiting predatory behavior. According to the Center for Wildlife Information, "Any bear . . . that continues to approach, follow, disappear and reappear, or displays other stalking behaviors is acting in a predatory manner." M. Sanjayan, a scientist for the Nature Conservancy, says "It's the way of all bears to practice sly and oblique approaches as a prelude to an attack." Bears will also turn sideways to show a larger profile, as a warning. My bear had given me a sideways view at both encounters. I thought nothing of it at the time.

More recently, I have learned that fully half of the fatal bear attacks in the United States and Canada during the past century were by black bears, who of course greatly outnumber brown and polar bears. More surprising are the results of a study of black bear attacks conducted by scientists at the University of Calgary and reported by Cheryl Lyn Dybas in *Natural History Magazine*:

> The team examined all sixty-three deaths in fifty-nine fatal incidents between 1900 and 2009

attributed to [wild black bears] in Canada and the U.S., including Alaska. Of fifty-six of those incidents in which they had sufficient information to analyze the attack, they determined that in forty-nine cases, or 88 percent, the attacking bear was exhibiting predatory behavior. In thirty-six of those attacks, the sex of the bear was conclusively known: thirty-three of those predators, or 92 percent, were male. A widespread assumption is that the riskiest encounter is with a mother bear with cubs, but in fact the bear to beware is a male looking for a meal.

For now, I'm going with the too-old-and-stringy hypothesis. My bear was an epicurean.

Center for Wildlife Information website. www.centerforwildlifeinformation.org

Winston Churchill. *The Story of the Malakand Field Force: An Episode of Frontier War.* Edinburgh: Thomas Nelson & Sons, 1916.

Cheryl Lyn Dybas. "A Frenzy of Bears." *Natural History Magazine* 119, no. 7 (July–August) 2011.

John Gimlette. *Theatre of Fish: Travels through Newfoundland and Labrador.* New York: Knopf, 2005.

MountainNature website. www.mountainnature.com

DUEL ON THE STRAIT

URING MY VISIT TO THE ISLAND OF NEWFOUNDLAND
in late summer 2011, remnants of two hurricanes
struck, and a third came ashore just after I left.
Newfoundlanders shrugged. The Cape Ray area near Port
aux Basques often has winds in excess of 120 miles per
hour, equivalent to Category 3 hurricanes. Those winds
used to blow the sarcastically named Newfie Bullet train
off its narrow-gauge tracks before it was permanently
blown off by construction of the cross-island highway and
freight-hauling trucks.

Nowadays, strong winds are mostly a bother to boats
and laundry. Boatmen stay ashore, except for crews on the
large ferries to and from Nova Scotia and Labrador. Those
vessels are part of the commercial highway and must set
against the wind—and sometimes, it seems, against reason.

Winds were strong along the Strait of Belle Isle during
the latter part of my stay in southern Labrador. A few days
before I departed, the Labrador ferry, *Apollo*, had set out
from St. Barbe, Newfoundland, for its two-hour crossing
to Blanc-Sablon, a small town in Quebec about a mile
from the Labrador border. Aboard the *Apollo* were some
high-ranking government officials, but the winds were too
strong to dock on the Quebec/Labrador side of the strait.
So the ferry loitered offshore, waiting for the gale to ebb.
But the wind wouldn't cooperate, and the vessel eventually
had to return to Newfoundland, a wasted six hours of
official lives.

(Those passengers got off easy. Two weeks later, the ferry from Nova Scotia to Newfoundland dawdled offshore for thirty-six hours before docking, thanks to the remnants of Hurricane Maria.)

A big part of the docking problem at Blanc-Sablon was that the *Apollo* had to back in. The ferry always nosed in to St. Barbe on the Newfoundland side, so cars and trucks heading to Labrador boarded through the bow. After backing in at Blanc-Sablon, the vehicles drove off through the stern. Backing in was a much more difficult maneuver than nosing in and required more power. Wind just made it worse.

The failed crossing with the high government officials was prominently noted by the region's weekly newspaper, the *Northern Pen*, the inspiration for the newspaper in Annie Proulx's novel *The Shipping News*. The *Pen* reported the *Apollo* was in need of repair and had been operating all summer at only 65 percent of its power capacity. During my own later crossing from Labrador to Newfoundland, I was told by a crew member that the vessel had to shut down the kitchen as well as all other nonessential power uses to gather enough thrust to perform the backing-in maneuver. It is possible the journey of those high government officials was thwarted by an overlooked toaster.

My plans were to leave Labrador on a Monday, but I had become so enamored of the little outport of Red Bay that I decided to stay two more days. It is well I did, because the Monday crossing I had originally reserved was canceled. Not just the crossing was canceled, but most of the day for those with reservations, due to the particulars of the ferry operation. Had I tried to depart Monday, I would have left Red Bay about 10 in the morning to arrive at the terminal in Blanc-Sablon by noon. The ferry was scheduled to leave at 1 p.m., and those with reservations had to check in at least an hour before departure. Arriving late not only forfeited the reservation, but incurred a $10 penalty euphemistically called a nonrefundable deposit.

On that Monday, the winds again were too strong for docking, and the *Apollo* meandered to and fro just offshore before finally giving up about 5 p.m. and returning to Newfoundland. During that time, those who were booked for the 1 p.m. crossing had to sit there and wait until the decision to abort was made. I would have wasted a day that could have been—and actually was—happily spent in Red Bay.

So instead I left Red Bay for Blanc-Sablon on Wednesday morning. The wind was mild and the forecast good. But by the time I got to the ferry terminal, the bluster had picked up again. Way up. The *Apollo* had not yet docked and could not be seen, as the strait was clotted with a fog as thick as pease pudding. I checked in at the terminal office, where no one knew what was going to happen. I was assured the *Apollo* was just offshore, out there in the pease pudding. I prepared myself for a lost day, splitting time between reading a book in the pickup and standing in the bluster on the edge of the wharf, looking for some sign of the ferry, some attempt by it to get close enough for us to cast our hope to one another.

And then, after an interminable and dismal wait, the *Apollo* slowly appeared out of the fog, an apparition in transit from phantom to matter, gathering detail real and imagined. At first it was the ghost ship of the *Flying Dutchman*, then a three-master 150 years late from a whaling voyage, and penultimately a World War II merchant vessel come in from its dance with a German submarine. The *Apollo* was all of these, beyond its allotted time, unable to dock, condemned to wander in sight of land as the wind and the captain stared each other down.

The afternoon wore on, and the wind actually strengthened, diminishing hope. But the captain did not blink. Instead, after two hours of posturing, he attempted to back in, despite what seemed a greater danger. Maybe it was the aftertaste of the failed crossing with the officials, or the subsequent bad press. Maybe it was a call from the owner, or a look from the first mate. Whatever it was, he did not blink. Heaving mightily against the wind, the captain swung *Apollo*'s stern to the Blanc-Sablon dock.

After the ferry unloaded its Labrador-bound traffic, we boarded and set off through the frothing strait for St. Barbe. I bought a 5-ounce cup of black tea at the cafeteria for $1.81. A refill cost as much. The tea was already brewed and came out of a 5-gallon container. A chronic tightwad, I tried to regard it as another contribution to the needed repairs. Nonetheless, the ferry owner was walking a fine line when he risked our safety <u>and</u> charged $1.81 for each small cup of generic tea. "It's the *Apollo*, for cod's sake," I told him in absentia, "not the *QE2*. Most of your passengers are out of work for half the year."

As soon as we were free of the Blanc-Sablon harbor, the *Apollo* began to lurch from side to side. We were exactly perpendicular to the wind and its battering waves. At first, it was just my tea cup accelerating across the table. But soon the vessel began to roll violently. Some people, having spent years of their lives on boats, thought they could walk but instead could only slam into bulkheads. Dishes and pots in the kitchen slid along counters and crashed to the deck. Doors banged open and shut. I threw life preservers to the fears that kept bobbing up in my mind of ships lost at sea.

As we got closer to Newfoundland, the wind hardly let up, but a bit of sun made its way through the fog, and little rainbows sailed above the waves reeling off *Apollo*'s bow.

"That was one of our roughest rides," a crew member said as we approached St. Barbe. But the young woman sitting at the next table disagreed.

"This happens all the time," she said. She worked for the school system and crossed over to Labrador every week. "It's always windy on the strait."

But rather than being a comfort, her words were a disappointment. I wanted it to be one of the worst rides ever. I had paid dearly for those fears, and she had reduced them to mere paranoia.

Annie Proulx. *The Shipping News.* New York: Scribner, 1994.

AN ESSAY IN WHICH PAM GRIER OOZES OUT OF HER CLOTHES

THE ATTENTION NEEDED FOR DRIVING CAN BE STRESSFUL even on quiet rural roads, and road-stop comfort food lives up to its name. I am particularly fond of maple bars while driving in the western United States. According to Wikipedia, where unproven assertions lurk in the interstices of legitimate research, maple bars are "a rectangular pastry topped with a maple glaze. It is a regional term from the Pacific Northwest, specifically Oregon and Washington. Elsewhere it is known as a maple-glazed Long John."

Although I have lived on the East Coast since the late 1960s, I have never seen a maple bar east of Delta, Utah. Frankly, I'd hesitate to put anything in my mouth with the words *Long John* in its name.

The nearest thing to a maple bar I have seen back east is the maple donut at Dunkin' Donuts. By comparison, the maple bar is elegant and aristocratic, with thrice the load of my sweet brown childhood opiate. The authentic version has the consistency of glazed rather than cakey donuts, is about six inches long and three inches wide, and more than an inch high. The maple topping is thick and soft like a frosting, not a hard, veneer-thin glaze.

While I was growing up in Portland, Oregon, circa 1950, a bakery truck made regular stops along our street. It was a highlight of my week and I knew the schedule well, rushing to the back of the truck as the driver gathered together a neighbor's order. (My family never ordered from the truck; Mom baked our pastries.)

"Got any empty maple bar sheets?" I'd ask. The bars were on sheets of wax paper large enough to hold about three dozen of the chewy rectangles. They were so fresh when placed on the wax paper at the bakery that some of the still-warm maple frosting ran down the sides of the bars and gathered in thick pools. As these heavenly excesses dried, they adhered to the wax paper, remaining after the bars had been removed. These were the lode of the maple sheet, whose final and most redeeming use was to line my belly, and my dentist's wallet.

"Got one just for you," said the bakery truck driver in the old movie that plays in my head. The sheet had to be handled carefully so no loose glops of maple frosting would fall to the street. Most glops continued to adhere to the sheet and were scraped off with the lower incisors. This childhood experience welded a lifelong romance with the maple bar that now has to endure long periods of absence with only brief reunions, like a sailor returning to his love between voyages.

A few years back, while gathering maple bars early one morning in a Portland Safeway store, I encountered another gatherer who like me was a maple bar exile, living in barren lands.

"Can't get these in Wisconsin," he said.

"Nor in North Carolina," said I. For a moment we were a spontaneous maple bar deprivation support group.

Tim Hortons is Canada's Dunkin' Donuts equivalent, likewise with a multitude of fresh-baked pastries, a coffee addictive to many, and a seemingly constant line of customers. Hortons also has a maple-frosted donut, called the maple dip, plus a borderline pornographic maple-frosted cream bun called a Canadian maple. But these are only stop-gaps for a maple bar, and each is tempered by its deficit.

Every summer I head from my home in North Carolina to the island of Newfoundland in eastern Canada. Coming up the island's west coast, there is no Tim Hortons between Deer Lake and St. Anthony, a distance of more than 250 miles. With a maple fix out of the question, local bakeries become an important source of alternative comforts. I have learned where they are—and sadly, where they used to be. Small businesses in Newfoundland come and go like road-side weeds.

Back in 2005, I found a bakery in Port au Choix run by an attractive woman with warm eyes and long brunette hair, maybe in her late forties. Her body expressed what I inter-preted to be a gentle enthusiasm for her product, headed in the direction of Pam Grier in the movie *Jackie Brown*. Pam is voluptuous to the point of oozing out of her clothes, a hu-man mocha cream pastry. Two years later the Port au Choix bakery was gone, leaving in its wake ungratified desire.

In February 2009, the bakery in Flowers Cove shut down its ovens. I had stopped there frequently, and its loss was a blow, the partridgeberry muffins particularly missed. Of all the government subsidies in the world, I can't think of a commercial enterprise more deserving than the independent neighborhood bakery.

In September 2009, I wasn't sure I would find a bakery along the Viking Trail highway north from Deer Lake. I had spent the night at Cow Head and was surprised to find a bakery just up the road in Parson's Pond. Like so many businesses in outport Newfoundland, it was nondescript, the front wall with one small window and a simple "Bakery" sign tucked up just below the eave. Its customers needed no other encouragement, and most lived within walking dis-tance. But I nearly missed it at 25 mph.

It was just past eight, early for Newfoundland, and there

wasn't much freshly baked to choose from. I settled for an unglazed cinnamon roll. I don't eat them often and avoid those that come with a thin and hard sink-white glaze.

Back on the road, this cinnamon roll turned out to be flakier than most, even a little crunchy, at least at the edges. It tended to crumble, raining crumbs on my shirt and crotch, so I set it on a napkin on the passenger seat and ate it by unrolling it, breaking off bite-size pieces.

I had barely crossed Parson's Pond River when the unrolled bits of pastry became a portal to the past. They had the taste and texture of the cinnamon strips my mom had made from purposefully leftover pie dough in the 1940s and '50s. She buttered the strips, sprinkled them with sugar and cinnamon, laid them crisscross on a pie tin, and baked them in the oven. I probably hadn't thought of them in more than half a century and was suddenly flooded with memories of my first home, especially from the kitchen. Mom continued to bake pies until she died, but I don't think she ever again made cinnamon strips after her children left home.

The cinnamon roll—thought to have been invented in Sweden, where October 4 is Cinnamon Roll Day—had potential as a maple bar proxy. It couldn't substitute for the oral qualities, but it might work for the spiritual ones. It became part of the morning hunt on road days.

The next day I had a cinnamon roll on the Strait of Belle Isle, out from St. Barbe on the *Apollo*, the two-hour ferry to Labrador. The roll, baked in the ferry's cafeteria, appeared to have been made in a hurry, or in too hot an oven, or with an improper apportioning of key ingredients. It looked like an old sandlot baseball, its cover unraveling like a great distended tongue stained with dark russet dirt.

The south coast of Labrador, from L'Anse au Clair north to Red Bay, is known as the Labrador Straits. It is culturally similar to the Newfoundland on the other side of the strait, having been settled mostly by the English, Scots, and Irish. The French, who used to fish there, left behind nothing but the names of a few towns, another being L'Anse au Loup.

With six hundred people, L'Anse au Loup was one of very few rural towns in the province of Newfoundland and Labrador that was actually growing in size during the first decade of the twenty-first century. This may have been due to its modern fishing facilities, to banking and other regional services, and to a generous public spirit. At the annual two-day L'Anse au Loup Days festival in August, meals were free and available to everyone. The town's several nonprofit organizations were staffed by more than a hundred volunteers, a significant percentage of the population.

And then there was Dot's Bakery and Coffee Shop, the only bakery I found in southern Labrador. Even the smell was fattening. There were the usual donuts, muffins, and tea biscuits; cookies, cakes, and pies; date squares and Nanaimos; things mingled, topped, or stuffed with partridgeberries and blueberries; loaves of bread, congregations of molasses buns. And the best cinnamon roll I have ever eaten. At first glance it appeared to have the detested sugar-hard white glaze. But a closer look revealed a thick and generous cream-colored frosting festooned with swirls and arcuate peaks, and coating a roll the size of a small continent.

"What kind of frosting is that on the cinnamon roll?" I asked the plump serving woman, her shape apparently an unavoidable consequence of working in this habitat.

"Cream cheese," she said with a shy smile and just a hint of mischief, as if she knew the power she held over men's lives.

On my way home to North Carolina, I stopped to visit friends on outer Cape Cod, where I had lived for two decades beginning in the late 1960s. I stayed in Provincetown, and each morning went to a backstreet grocery store that had great coffee, pastries, and a few places to sit and socialize, read, or open a laptop. During my first morning at the grocery, the baker came out of the kitchen with a large tray of pastries. We looked at each other with great surprise and delight. She was a friend I had known since the 1970s but had seen only once in the past twenty years. I got up, she set down the tray, and we warmly embraced, swaying side to side. She invited me back to the kitchen to talk while she worked.

"Remember our trip to New Hampshire?" she asked.

"Of course."

"It's a good memory," she said, smiling.

During the first years of my time in Provincetown, we had not been close friends but, rather, part of a community of friends, a fellowship. In those days, some forty years ago, she had a small seasonal business, and once a month I balanced her books. One day she asked me if I would help her deliver an order to New Hampshire. Neither of us was in a relationship at the time, and the two-day trip became a romantic interlude that continues to be a good memory for me, and as it turns out, for her as well. Although it didn't result in an outward change in our relationship, the adventure brought us closer together. From then on, there was a comfortable feeling of familiarity in our everyday encounters that has continued to the present, in spite of long absences.

As we spoke of old friends and new lives, she continued her baking. Laid out on the large metal table in front of her was a great rectangle of dough. She brushed melted butter over the entire surface, then added sugar and—what else?— cinnamon. Making a small fold in the long edge nearest her, she rolled the rectangle into a long beige log nearly half a foot in diameter.

"I can't believe you're making cinnamon rolls," I said. "They became part of the adventure on this trip to New-foundland," and I told her about the pastry pilgrimage that began with Mom's pie dough strips recalled by the roll from Parson's Pond. There was a bit of magic at work in my old friend's kitchen that morning, and two very good memories.

PART IV.

PAST REMEMBERING

These stories are all faithful to memory, but I can't verify that memory remains faithful to truth. (The above title stands by its double entendre.) A few of the memories are quite distant, more than sixty years old, and may have been smudged here and there by the long wait. In places I have forgotten a name, but that is often just as well, possibly saving me from a beating or lawsuit. As I say elsewhere in these pages, a lot of fiction is just memoir in a witness protection program.

My literary career began in 1961, when I changed my college major from journalism to English literature. It ended three years later when I got a C in an evening poetry class. Nonetheless, it took me another two decades before I finally gave up the dream of becoming a "creative" writer. I am fortunate to have freed a writing voice so late in life.

From Snitch to Scab

I BEGAN MY NEWSPAPER CAREER AS A SNITCH, AGE NINE, in 1950. We lived on the northern edge of Portland, Oregon, only three blocks from the cutover bottomlands between the city and the Columbia River. This intermittently flooded wasteland had been partially filled by railroad beds, stockyards, and disposal areas for industrial waste. To a boy of nine, it was a frontier with high potential for treasure (some of it toxic), and one afternoon I found it. Down at the foot of a railroad embankment were hundreds of advertising circulars all rolled up like small newspapers.

There was no value in the circulars themselves. The treasure lay in how they got there. They were supposed to have been delivered house to house by a boy on a bicycle. I figured he had tossed them like a dead body into the early morning miasma. Delivering advertising circulars was a coveted job, one of the few a child could legally do. I took home a piece of the evidence, and Dad called the distributor. I was quickly rewarded with the miscreant's job.

The circulars were supposed to be delivered in the early morning once a week. Some guy in a truck dumped a large bale of them on our front porch after midnight. Mom had to get up an hour before me to start rolling the hundreds of circulars so I could toss them on porches like the professional paperboys did. But even with her help there was not enough time to complete the deliveries before breakfast and school.

I wasn't about to devote another morning to the task,

let alone a precious afternoon, so it wasn't long before I realized the practicality of the snitched-on boy's method. I began to deliver to as many houses as time allowed, then hid the overburden in more secluded areas of the wasteland. The bodies were never found, so I continued distribution of the circulars to the local neighborhood and bottomlands until I finally got a job delivering real newspapers at age eleven.

(There is a parallel between the start of my newspaper career and the beginning for a politician: tear down the unscrupulous incumbent, then discover the job can't be done by scruple alone. "Politics," observed socialist Oscar Ameringer, "is the gentle art of getting votes from the poor and campaign funds from the rich, by promising to protect each from the other.")

In the early 1950s, Portland had two dailies: the morning *Oregonian* and the evening *Oregon Journal.* My first newspaper job was delivering the *Journal* in late afternoon, after school. The paperboys gathered at the newspaper's district distribution center, a sturdy shack at the back of a supermarket parking lot. We had to be there before the newspaper truck arrived, so there was always time to kill, and the favorite place to kill it was in the supermarket's candy section. Our goal was to shoplift as many candy bars as possible under the ruse of the purchase of one or two. Once outside, we tallied and compared the sweet ephemera.

The nickel-and-dime thievery was of course perilous, and every now and then one of us was caught. But for my group of preteen boys in the early 1950s, shoplifting was only a risky option, not the beginning of a wasted life. Better behavior had to compete with peer pressure, unenlightened self-interest, and the inherent goodness of a Baby Ruth candy bar. Most important, shoplifting reduced the drawdown of wealth I was acquiring for a bicycle upgrade.

(At the time, I was only interested in the money I was making and gave no thought to the economic system that newspaper delivery represents. We were little franchises. The newspapers themselves were actually being sold to the paperboys, not to the subscribers. Once a month the company handed us a bill, and we collected from the subscribers to pay it. The remainder was ours. Any unpaid account was the paperboy's problem. He not only got no profit on those accounts but had to pay the company for the papers he had delivered to the scofflaws. Yet even with the economic assistance of eleven-year-old boys, printed newspapers appear headed for oblivion.)

I became a newspaperman during my senior year of high school, when I discovered that calculus and girls couldn't be studied at the same time. Getting girls to make out requires effort and focus when competition, pursuit, and anxiety are factored in. I abandoned my dream of becoming a geologist exploring for oil in Venezuela and amended my curriculum by replacing lonely and cerebral calculus with a very sociable course in journalism. The journalism class was responsible for writing and publishing the school newspaper. I loved sports and got the plum job of sports editor, even though I wasn't much of an athlete, breaking my arm the first time I tried to swing on rings.

One of my responsibilities after a varsity game was to call the *Oregonian* and the *Oregon Journal* to relate the score and a few highlights. That year our football team was very good, and I had kept track of statistics for each player. I began getting phone calls from the *Oregonian* reporter who covered high school athletics. He wanted those statistics for his weekly column. After a couple of months, he asked me if I would be interested in the most stupendous offer anyone had ever made to me: a one-night-a-week job as a bottom-rung copy writer at the downtown *Oregonian* building itself, in the exalted sports department.

At first, I just worked Friday evenings. That was game night. Several of us were there to answer phone calls from informants, record the scores and highlights, *and write a two- or three-sentence account of the game.* My literary career was airborne.

Following high school, I enrolled as a journalism major at Pacific University in Forest Grove, about thirty miles west of Portland. I kept working part-time for the *Oregonian,* adding Tuesday and Saturday nights to my schedule.

Thanks to the business world's chronic cost cutting, I was about to get even more work. The newspapers had recently automated another part of the printing process, causing a 75 percent reduction in the number of workers needed among members of the Stereotypers Union. In November 1959, the stereotypers went on strike, and members of other unions refused to cross the picket lines.

Managers of both newspapers huddled in the *Oregonian* building and attempted to print their dailies with nonunion help. Tempers flared when nonunion workers crossed the picket lines. There were fights. A newspaper delivery van was blown up. Then the managing editor of the sports department called and asked me to be part of the nonunion publishing team, with a full-time job. I crossed the picket line with a bodyguard: Dad. My career had entered the scab phase.

> After God had finished the rattlesnake, the toad, and the vampire, he had some awful substance left with which he made a scab. A scab is a two-legged animal with a corkscrew soul, a water brain, a combination backbone of jelly and glue. Where others have hearts, he carries a tumor of rotten principles. When a scab comes down the street, men turn their backs and Angels weep in Heaven, and the devil shuts the gates of hell to keep him out.
> —*attributed to Jack London, probably erroneously*

Whoever wrote it, they were wrong about my having rotten principles. I had no principles, and no politics either, so by default was a Republican like my dad. I had been convinced that crossing the picket line was the right thing to do, even though I felt guilty for it. I continued crossing the line uneasily for another two years. (The strike lasted five years before the unions finally gave up.)

Every now and then, as I crossed the picket line, I would see the reporter who had recruited me from high school. He never spoke to me, but his gaze conveyed admonishment and deep disappointment. It is a gaze that still haunts me, and in my own mythology it was the beginning of another way to view the world.

A Beautiful Lie

P ETS IN OUR HOUSE WERE SHORT-LIVED WHILE I WAS
growing up in Portland, Oregon, in the 1940s. As
in most houses, we failed to read the labels carefully,
and the fishes, frogs, turtles, birds, and dogs found themselves in an environment where improvisation and tough
love were the functional equivalents of natural selection.
Only the guppies prospered, something of a miracle, as
they were under my care. I must have assisted in the live
birth of a thousand newborn, transferring them from tank
to tank so they would not be eaten by the adults. That may
be the ultimate measure of fecundity, that you can afford to
eat your young. We are on track with overpopulation and
Christianity's symbolic cannibalism: communion.

One of my earliest memories is watching in horror as
Mom flushed a dead goldfish down the toilet. We thought
it had died from overfeeding. I think she let me watch as a
life lesson. Things live, things die, you flush the toilet and
move on.

The first real tragedy was the baby chicken. There were
two of them, mine and my sister's, and they managed to
stay alive with us for a few weeks. One day Mom, the
chicks, and I were out back working in the garden, Mom
shoveling while I helped the chickens find bugs in the
freshly overturned soil. Mom had her mind on the garden
and didn't see the little chicken—my little chicken—behind
her as she stepped back. It squeaked loudly, and blood
oozed from the base of its beak. Mom instantly put it out

of its misery and into mine with a forceful whack of the
shovel. A quick burial followed. I ran into the house and
bawled all the way to my bedroom. Another death, another tough lesson: mothers can kill the things you love.
Only in adulthood could I appreciate her grit. She was the
daughter of farmers.

The *überpet*, the one who became a beloved family
member, was Mike the dog. We found him one evening
as we pulled into the driveway. There he sat in the head-
lights, as if he had been waiting for us, eyes wide, but not
startled. He looked like a wolf pup, maybe six weeks old,
mostly German shepherd with a dash of collie, or so we
surmised. He had no collar. We gave him water, and he
was still there in the morning.

Sis and I pleaded to keep him, offering to perform
all required maintenance. Dad and Mom relented, as they
were quickly taken by him too. No one ever came to claim
him. He must have been cast off from an unwanted or
too-large litter.

Like all wolves, he was a pack animal. Mike knew that
Mom and Dad were the alpha dogs, and Sis and I were
more or less his equals, though she and I had far too
many unfair privileges. Like who got to sit at the dinner
table and who didn't. He slept at night in the basement,
behind a closed door. I was the first one up most mornings, and the day began with a dog fight. I went to the
basement first thing, where Mike and I would wrestle
on the cement floor. We were fairly equal in applied
strength—that is, neither of us tried to maim or kill the
other—but his weapons were sharper than mine. Most
days I went to school with scratches and bites on my fore-
arms and hands. They were badges.

Mike's pack behavior ultimately was his doom. He had
to be restrained in the presence of strangers. It took several
visits for him to accept friends of the family, and their

arrival was always greeted with an attack-mode bark. He
barked at passersby on the sidewalk and was under restraint outdoors. Mom tried to rid him of this quite natural
territorial behavior with a rolled-up newspaper and whacks
to his long nose.

But his instincts were too strong. Outside, he would
bark as viciously as he could and then immediately assume
a defensive position, sprawled on the ground, both front
paws covering his nose even before Mom came out of the
house with the rolled-up newspaper. What intelligence that
reveals: remembered experience, anticipation, cause and
effect, predicting another creature's behavior.

One day Mike got loose and bit a passerby. The victim
reported the incident to the police, and that evening two
patrolmen came to the door. Mike did a terrible job of
arguing his innocence and was led to the basement. Sis
and I were shooed out of the living room. After the police
left, we were told the verdict. Guilty. Mike had been sentenced to the dog pound. Sis and I were too young
to know what that meant.

The next morning, Mom and Dad took Mike to the
pound while we kids were in school. When we got home,
we could see that Mom had been crying, maybe all day.

A few days later, Dad told us a beautiful lie. He said
he had called the dog pound and found that Mike had
been adopted by the owner of a ranch in eastern Oregon.
Many nights followed with me thinking of him running
with the horses and cows, of endless plains and hills where
barks could be hurled with impunity. And for a long time,
even into my adulthood, he would return in a dream, the
first of lost loved ones to do that.

ELVIS

M Y EARLIEST MUSICAL MEMORIES COME FROM THE basement of our house in Portland, where Dad had his photography darkroom, and I had a nook where I worked on my stamp collection. It was late 1940s into early 1950s. As we hobbied, Dad listened to his big band albums and to crooners like Bing Crosby and Jo Stafford. It became my music by default, and it can still punch me sixty-five years later—not so much the music itself, but the powerful memories rooted in it.

Popular music was just about to turn a corner and leave Dad's big bands and crooners behind. It was getting younger, grittier, sexier, more emotional, even angst-driven. It grew out of Black rhythm and blues. It was rock 'n' roll. Bill Haley and the Comets introduced us White folks to it in 1954 with "Shake, Rattle and Roll" and "Rock Around the Clock."

But the first song to turn the corner and tell us there was no going back was Elvis Presley's "Heartbreak Hotel," in the winter of early 1956. I was fourteen, and Mom and I had walked two blocks for lunch at the new fast-food hamburger joint. We ordered 19-cent hamburgers—cheap even then—and sat in plastic chairs at a Formica-topped table. It was all so modern.

Suddenly this wild new sound came from the burger joint's speakers, like nothing we had heard before. A White man was singing rock 'n' roll like a Black man. He was singing hard-knocks rock. Not only had Elvis turned the corner, he'd gone down to the end of Lonely Street and took us with him. It was revolution by music. The world would never be the same.

When Bob Dylan paid tribute to the most influential rock stars of that era in a March 2015 AARP interview, he mentioned everyone but Elvis. I thought it was an incredible omission that not even old age could excuse. Maybe Dylan was not able to reconcile Las Vegas casino shows or all those silly movies. But it was Elvis who hit rock 'n' roll out of the park and around the world on January 27, 1956. Even my mom, an ancient thirty-three, became an instant fan. I'll bet Dylan was too, for a while.

Touching God

ROBERTA WAS A HOMECOMING PRINCESS. I WAS A non-athletic math and science nerd, and forever grateful she went against custom. Furtive glances in the high school hallways led to flirtatious smiles, and one evening I summoned the nerve to park in front of her house. That was an accepted dating technique in Portland circa 1958. I was seventeen and driving my first car, a 1947 Chevy fastback. Paid a hard-earned $75 for it. It looked supercool parked in front of Roberta's house, the light from the streetlamp shimmering off its sloping back. She came out of the house, and I invited her to sit in the car with me. To my relief and terror, she did.

That began a courtship consisting mostly of short trips to the A&W Root Beer drive-in after dusk. For guys, the drive-in dates showed that someone had found us desirable, and that one of the highest status symbols for boys on Planet High School was within reach: sexual intercourse. The drive-in visits were followed by curbside make-out sessions in front of her house. This falsely reassured her parents of no bad behavior.

Adolescent passion in Chevy fastbacks was a fumbling of buttons, buckles, and bra hooks, with forays into unfathomed territories portending incomparable wealth or loss. Night after night, our passion ended in a standoff. But as time went on, her defenses weakened, and I stood a little closer. I was obsessed with losing my virginity to a woman who was under considerable pressure not to lose hers. She

and her family belonged to a fundamentalist church, the
Wesleyan Methodists. My upbringing was among ordinary
Methodists, whose pilgrimage relied more on homily than
on fire and brimstone.

And so it came to pass that the desire to fornicate
brought me to the Wesleyan Sunday services, where you
could actually smell and feel the heat of hell. The charismatic preacher was a magnificent orator, beginning with a
few daily temptations and the lies we tell ourselves. Before
you knew it, the congregation was bound for a tour of
the devil's realm, with fire and brimstone everywhere. The
preacher's face, puffy even when calm, was blood-red,
drenched in sweat, and swollen near to bursting. "Amen!"
escaped from old men like vented steam, fanning the
preacher's fire. At times I thought he was going to have
a stroke as he bellowed warnings and predictions of the
soul's imminent demise. And then his voice would soften
as he delivered our only hope, God's eternal love and forgiveness, a pillow held out to catch us in our fall. To those
caught, it was spiritual euphoria.

After Sunday church, the congregation gathered at
the home of one of the families for a potluck. By then
the preacher's furnaces had cooled. The oral violence,
the threats and accusations, had been stored for the next
flame-throwing sermon. Away from the brimstone, he was
one of the sweetest men I ever met. The radiance stream-
ing from his face could only have come from the constant
touch of God.

God touched me at the Wesleyan summer camp. I had
already been to the camps run by the ordinary Methodists, where grace before meals, a few bible readings, and
prayers before bed were the only required stops on our
spiritual journey. Roberta had invited me to attend the
Wesleyan camp, and I had agreed, not wanting to jeopar-
dize the course my sex drive had mapped out. The

Wesleyan camp had daytime crafts and physical activities like the ordinary Methodists had, but evenings were different. Each night we gathered in a Quonset hut auditorium for the saving of our souls, and each night we heard a new voice. The camp recruited its attendees from a large region, and with them came a phalanx of preachers for the calling out of ripening young sinners.

To that point in my life, church had been a Sunday routine, and I regarded myself as religious. Church attendance had been required of me and my sister from early childhood, but our parents only attended on Christmas and Easter. (At the time, I was critical of them for this apparent hypocrisy.) Besides the Sunday services, I attended weekly classes for children and later for adolescents. These classes also served critical secular needs, as it was here I first encountered girls socially, out of school. I had my first dance at a church social, and later my first kiss, an awkward bumping of lips in the bushes beneath a stained-glass window. By the time I started dating Roberta, sex and religion were already intertwined. But I believed in God and had proof of His existence even before I attended the Wesleyan camp meeting.

Earlier that year, a friend and I had driven the fastback out into the hinterland of Sauvie Island, forty square miles of dikes, farms, and bottomlands at the confluence of the Willamette and Columbia rivers. My friend and I were of the opinion that adventure was more likely to be found by following the unpaved roadbeds on top of the dikes to the most remote parts of the island. It was a self-fulfilling opinion, as we eventually came to a place where part of the roadbed on top of the dike had washed out. After stopping to conduct a thorough engineering analysis, we got back in the car and abruptly nosed into the far wall of the washout, hopelessly stuck miles not only from home but from the nearest farmhouse.

It was a horrible situation, and I didn't know what was worse, leaving or staying. It would be a long walk back and require the abandoning of the beloved fastback. I feared it would be brutalized and pillaged, the fate of abandoned cars. And even if we got help in time, the towing fee would bankrupt me. The only positive option I could think of was divine intervention. So I walked off a little ways by myself, got down on my knees, and begged for deliverance. I promised God to do His bidding the rest of my life if He would only rescue the fastback from its terrible predicament.

As I walked back to the site of the disaster, I saw something moving on top of the dike at a great distance, maybe a mile away. It was another car, coming from the opposite direction, from the most remote part of the island. As it approached, I could hardly believe my eyes. Attached to the front bumper was something I had never seen on a sedan before: a cable winch. It was a miracle, my miracle, in answer to prayer less than five minutes old. God must have been hard up for new workers. There was no other reasonable explanation.

From that event until the Wesleyan camp meeting, I had not been particularly busy on behalf of God. It might even appear I was hard at work for the other guy. The Miracle of Sauvie Island had been reduced to intermittent moments of guilt lacquered with lame promises. But I think it was that incident more than anything else that primed me for the camp meeting's preacher-of-the-night. My journey on the Road to Damascus, as well as on the road to coitus, began in the fastback.

I don't remember the details of the preacher's exhortation, but I do remember the lighting. It was semidark where we sat on folding chairs in the Quonset hut, while up front the fluorescent light was glaring—not the sort of light associated with parting clouds and throngs of angels,

but of Quonset huts. It was almost too functional, showing
the interior of the building to be wholly without character
except for a small cross and framed picture of Jesus on
the wall behind the preacher. Whatever one might think of
fundamentalists, they are less concerned with the material.

At some point during the sermon—as usual, hot from
the fires of hell and the burning love of God—the visceral
words scoured the lacquer from my guilt-ridden soul. I felt
a power in me not mine responding to the preacher's bidding. It pulled me up out of the chair and to the front of
the hall, where I was so overwhelmed with Spirit I started
crying. A few others had also come forward, and for each
of us there was a preacher waiting. They were intimate
with the experience and would be our guide. Mine led me
back down the aisle to the door. But outside, he let the
Spirit move me, and I felt drawn to the area behind the
hut, near the wall closest to the sermonizer. I was euphoric, filled with God's love and forgiveness, crying from pure
joy, kneeling on the ground, leaning forward on my hands,
gushing happy tears in near-total darkness.

Suddenly, on the ground in front of me, within a foot
of my knees, there was a small circle of white light, no
more than two inches in diameter. Everything else was
black night, and the light made no sense according to
the known laws of the universe. It seemed not to have an
earthly origin, as if it had been beamed from heaven.

My guide was kneeling beside me, his arm draped
over my shoulders. I kept babbling on about this light, and
he finally said, "It's coming through that knothole in the
wall." Maybe he was tiring of my obsessiveness and wanted me to move on, taking a chance that a little ordinary
reality wouldn't hurt the mystical process. And it didn't.
Rather than deflate the moment, that too became part of
the mystery. I had been carried to that bit of ground by an
external force and had not seen the small circle of light

until after I had knelt down. It was no less of an experience because God had used humble elements of His universe—the Quonset hut's knothole and fluorescent lighting—to show me He was listening. He had made it tangible.

The experience was so strong the euphoria survived sleep and lingered well into the next day. I was in a state of bliss, with a constant radiant smile.

There was something of ecstasy in the mystical experience, and in retrospect it had properties that seem related to those of the aftermath of the sexual climax, as if they share a common physiological origin or pathway. In the euphoria following the sexual climax, I have sometimes experienced a strong sense that I have stepped outside of the limits of time, that my partner and I exist in an eternal realm as well as in a finite one—and in that eternal realm, the moment will continue forever. Although the content of the postclimax euphoria may vary widely among individuals (and within individuals), the euphoric sense of timelessness is probably a universal human capacity.

Unlike medieval troubadours, a charismatic evangelist might bristle at equating the sexual climax with the touch of God. But the preacher's argument is compromised by his own charisma. Whether emanating from him, a rock star, or Bill Clinton, charisma is subtly to overtly charged with sexual as well as spiritual energy. And charisma affects the self as well as the other. It is no wonder so many preachers fall by the wayside.

After camp, I continued going to church with Roberta and may even have uttered a few involuntary amens. But like the aftermath of the miracle on the dike, there was no follow-up labor for the Lord. Eventually, even the mystical experience became material, the organic high against which all future euphorias would be measured.

In his book *The Varieties of Religious Experience: A Study in Human Nature*, philosopher and psychologist William James demonstrates the mystical state to be a universal human attribute, available to all peoples and religions, and not the province of a particular set of beliefs. Though the prerequisites can differ, the experience is essentially the same for all: euphoria, the overwhelming presence of a supernatural power, a flood of revelations and insights, and feelings that cannot be described in words. The experience commonly lasts for an hour or two. Euphoria, ineffability, and a supernatural presence were strong characteristics of my Quonset hut experience, but I have no recollection of revelations and insights. Too bad—I would love to know now what was revelatory to my seventeen-year-old self.

James was never able to experience the natural mystical state. But he did experiment with nitrous oxide, which led him to conclude that "our normal waking consciousness ... is but one especial type of consciousness, whilst all about it, parted from it by the filmiest of screens, there lie potential forms of consciousness entirely different."

Although a large subculture has experimented with psychotropic substances since the 1960s, the natural mystical state in America today seems primarily confined to practitioners of evangelical religions. The experience may be most accessible as a "calling out" within a group setting. Thanks to the televangelists, many nonevangelicals no doubt view the natural mystical state as temporary insanity at best, and fraud at worst. Others may have an elitist view: Mahatma Gandhi was a mystic, but Mrs. Jones down the street is merely out of her mind.

A dozen years after my natural high, I began experimenting with acid (LSD) and psilocybin mushrooms. These produced amazing states of mind, including a sense of contact with the supernatural. But it was not an experience of God, at least not in the Christian sense. Instead, I felt I had risen to a higher realm of awareness, of feeling, of being. The mystical state without pretext and preparation. But it wasn't pure. Along with the experience of the supernatural were bouts with paranoia and episodes of fantastic images and perceptions—hallucinations— ultimately having little or nothing to do with a spiritual journey, at least for me. And the return to earth was often accompanied by a debilitating depression, opposite the feelings I experienced coming down from the natural high.

The closest I have come with chemistry to the natural high is with James's vehicle, nitrous oxide. In the dentist's chair. The first time was the most spiritual. I rose to a realm so high the worst imaginable thing was reconciled. For me in the early 1980s, that was nuclear holocaust. It was reconciled in an infinite place above the horror, where the universe always rights itself. As in the natural mystical state, I was aware of a supernatural presence that can be experienced but not described, except by metaphor. It is a realm where the urge to live is in the rocks, where life is the universe experiencing itself.

Every now and then I would descend to the dentist's chair to see how he was progressing. I was so euphoric that I hoped he had plenty of work left to do, and in those days he did, as my mouth had become a silver mine of cavities, crowns, and root canals. With the prospect of more nitrous oxide, it was a struggle to take better care of my teeth.

In the experience, the supernatural presence is immediate, infinite, and unknowable. Call it God or not. Whatever it is, the mystical state has no doubt of its existence. The experience and its realm may be confined to our individuality, but the experience itself argues the opposite.

The mystical state is a psychophysiological capacity residing in all of us, a component of our being, like thumbs and laughter. It could have evolved from another purpose, another psychophysiological function, the sexual climax, our most accessible path to a natural euphoria.

From my perspective, it took a lifetime to reach the maturity needed to write about these events. I am fortunate that aspects of the mystical experience feel as fresh now as when they happened. Roberta and I broke up before graduation and never saw each other after high school. She married and had children, then died too soon, in the late 1980s. But she is still in that long-ago memory, and somewhere we are in an eternal moment forever.

William James. *The Varieties of Religious Experience: A Study in Human Nature.* New York: Longmans, Green, 1902.

Mentor of Cool

THERE WERE BEATNIKS AND WANNABES LIKE ME IN 1959 Portland coffeehouses. We sipped espressos and listened to cool jazz, whatever that was. Too young and inexperienced to distinguish authentic from pretentious, I tried, impossibly, to be cool.

Then cool came to me. My dad had candy machines at several scattered locations around the city, including a record store in the heart of Albina, the ironically named Black neighborhood in North Portland. For a while during my senior year of high school I serviced the machines for him.

The odor of marijuana smoke saturated the record store, and the owner always had a smile beneath his Duke Ellington mustache. He asked me if I ever listened to jazz. I said Dad had an album of Benny Goodman's *Sing, Sing, Sing*, but that was about it, except for whatever was going on in the coffeehouses. He said, "Listen to this," and played me something by the Ramsey Lewis Trio. He moved his hands gracefully in the music, as if it were a fluid. He was guiding me, teaching me how to listen. And then I heard it.

He sold me the album at discount and introduced me to another each time I serviced the candy machines. He never pressured me to buy, but when I did, it was always at discount. I was sure no White boy in North Portland had more Ramsey Lewis and Ahmad Jamal albums than I did. I like to think my mentor of cool prized a White boy convert, a stone he had thrown to make ripples.

THE MAN INSIDE THE EFFIGY

NOT UNTIL HIS FUNERAL DID I BEGIN TO REALIZE how much of Dad's life I had misjudged. I was too busy rebelling, even at age thirty-seven, which is how old I was when he died on his sixty-first birthday.

But I got a glimpse of the man I couldn't see when several members of a Japanese American family unexpectedly attended his funeral. We had no idea who they were, or why they were there.

One of us Euro-American mourners approached them after the service, and we learned the Japanese American family had owned a grocery store in our Portland neighborhood. But it had been more than twenty-five years since we had moved away from the area, and thirty-four years since the incident that prompted their attendance at his funeral.

During World War II, they had been forced to relocate from Portland to an internment camp. (Imprisoning families of other ethnicities is another measure of our chronic barbarism.) After their release in 1945, Dad was the first to welcome them home. It seems a simple act, yet it had great meaning for them, and their gratitude lasted his lifetime.

This was the man the Japanese American family saw, and it is to them that I owe the prompt for a larger view of his life.

GOING TO HELL WITH LAUREL AND HARDY

AFTER SPENDING THE SUMMER OF 1965 IN THE PEA fields of Skagit Valley, my wife and I returned to Seattle so I could continue my studies at the University of Washington. We moved into a small apartment above a third-rate auction house, where dump-worthy household goods pleaded for a last reprieve. The pea fields hadn't made us wealthy, and for a period of weeks we were destitute. There was a stretch of days where all we had to eat was a cauldron of kidney beans cooked with an onion and made more or less palatable with ketchup.

The auction happened every Saturday night and was great free entertainment. It wasn't long before the owners asked me if I wouldn't mind helping out for pay. The beans, onion, and ketchup give some hint of my answer. At first I helped top bidders load their vehicles with the furniture and other items they had acquired. Then the owners invited me to join them in their life of crime.

I have long forgotten the names of the two men who owned the enterprise. The heavyset auctioneer would have made a serviceable Oliver Hardy at a costume party. He was always either sullen or, if in a good mood, gloomy. During the auction, he was the opposite of what you would expect of a low-flying auctioneer. There was never any rapid-fire "Hey-do-I-hear-35-35-35? Thirty, going-once, 30, going-twice...." Instead, he voiced an indolent drawl, as if he were there against his will.

Shortly after I began working for them, Hardy confided

to me that "the bidding has to start low to get it moving. But there are some things we can't sell below a certain price, so what I need you to do is to stand there in the back like always and raise your bidding card to make sure those items don't sell for less than their value." He was asking me to be a shill. The dishonesty made me uncomfortable, but not enough to say no.

This new duty more than doubled my Saturday night work time. All I had to do was periodically raise my bidding card and faux-purchase a few relatively expensive items each auction. Some of those same items would be up for bid the following Saturday, and I might have to "buy" a few of them again. I began to get suspicious looks from the regulars and would have been easy pickings for some regulating authority's undercover agent.

The auctioneer didn't help matters. He was a terrible actor, and every time it was necessary for me to raise my bidding card, his vocal tone changed as he called out my bid. He sounded insincere, as if he were announcing the bid of a shill. Hardy was lousy at being a criminal.

Laurel, the other owner, was a much better actor: smooth, laid back, bemused—and beneath it all, a slime-bag. He had spent ten years in a military prison for peddling black-market cigarettes as a soldier in France after the end of World War II. Laurel took care of the supply end of the auction house, which was also a used furniture store between Saturday nights. My prowess as a shill must have been impressive, as I was soon accompanying Laurel in his truck to deliver sold furniture and pick up more used furniture.

I quickly learned that I was sinking to a much lower depth with Laurel than shilling ever could have taken me. In the morning, he would be sitting in their office reading the newspapers, scanning the obituaries for housefuls of furniture that might have to be sold quickly and cheaply.

On the phone, he was sympathetic, offering a service: "There are so many things that have to be taken care of when a family member passes on. Give us a call if the furniture has to be sold. We will be glad to help in this time of need."

I was appalled, but once again not enough to say no. My moral compass in this Dickensian world only had enough power to see where I was heading, none to alter course. It was all quite legal, but I had much more reason to feel guilty as a carrion-feeder than as a shill. When we went to the houses of the deceased to cart away the furniture, there were always bereaved family members present. I tried to look no one in the eye, working hard with Laurel to get out of there as quickly as possible. The price paid for the possessions hardly elevated the act above burglary in broad daylight.

I can—and do—attribute my almost casual acceptance of immoral behavior and laughable criminality to the ignorance of youth. Laurel and Hardy opened my eyes to the underside of commerce, to the deception, and to the erosion of morality—not just by greed but also by the insecurity that underlies fulfilling the day-to-day necessities of life.

AMERICAN TIMBUKTU

W HEN DAD DIED IN 1979, I INHERITED A FAMILY
tradition. For the next two decades, I headed
to Nevada once a year to play blackjack. Gambling had become an important element of our family life,
especially in the relationship between Dad and Mom, and
after he died, between Mom and me. Curiously, it was
not an addiction, at least not one resulting in great losses
of money, time, and self-respect. That moderating quality
came with the inheritance.

Dad was only eight when his mother died, and seventeen when his father died, in 1935. Dad had planned to attend a technical school and become an electronics wizard.
He loved radios and built them from scratch using recipes
in *Popular Mechanics*. But his father's death put technical
school out of reach economically, so one of his uncles got
him a job in the parts department of a Chevrolet dealer-
ship in Portland.

Ambitious, Dad soon became a Chevrolet salesman.
It was stressful, but he was good at it and won several
monthly and annual sales awards. He was sales manager
for a while, but a perforated ulcer sent him back to the
lesser stress of selling cars.

Once a year Dad piled us into the latest Chevy and we
drove off into the summer vacation. These began in 1946,
when I was five. That year was the first full summer after
the war. The vacations continued into the late 1950s. We
headed to great western sceneries, never straying farther

east than Utah and Arizona. At some point during the trip we always went to California, where we had relatives, and to Nevada, where we didn't.

The lure of Nevada was gambling. Looking back, it seems a great contradiction in Dad's character, as he was both pound- and penny-wise. But he had a strike-it-rich streak in him, which probably came from growing up in hard times. Panning for gold in Oregon and California creeks and rivers was another expression of it. This he also did in moderation, more of a hobby than an obsession.

It wasn't until he died that we discovered he had been investing his sales commissions in the stock market. Money had been so tight in our household that for a long time it felt like we were only one missed paycheck away from the soup kitchen. During my first dozen years, we didn't seem to be keeping up with the Joneses so much as trying to stay ahead of the African American families who lived a few blocks away in public housing built during the war. We were almost the last ones on the block to get a television. It was easy to tell, because in those days everyone with a TV had an antenna on the roof. Like the car in the driveway, it was a measure of perceived wealth, an enormous status symbol, the aluminum totem.

Back in the era before cars had air-conditioning (or before our car had air-conditioning), Nevada's parched landscape made oases of even the dingiest desert towns. Eventually, we visited nearly every one of those American Timbuktus with their legendary hotel-casinos: the Stockmen's in Elko, the Nevada in Ely, the Mizpah in Tonopah. For some reason, Las Vegas was never on the itinerary. Maybe it was geographically inconvenient. Maybe we were afraid of Bugsy Siegel.

But it was Reno we would return to and stay for more

than a night each visit. Our Mecca was the now-deceased Harold's Club, the largest casino in Nevada in the 1940s. The amount of Old West memorabilia made it like a museum, at least to a boy enthralled by Western legend. It was also family-friendly, with a small theater that continuously showed comedies, cartoons, and Westerns. The free movies functioned as daycare for parents who came to gamble. All of us could hardly wait to get there.

The only time children were allowed in the casino proper was when they were being escorted by parents to some nongambling area like a restaurant. It was thrilling to walk among what was forbidden anywhere else in the country: the noisy slot machines and rows of blackjack tables; the sunken hieroglyphic surfaces and gangster allure of the crap tables; the risk-it-all seduction of the roulette wheel. Everyone was smoking and drinking. It may have been the loosest town in America. Nevada had resurrected the Old West's aura of lawlessness, and bits of the Old West still got drunk there and wasted a month of wages there.

Growing up in Portland was not to grow up in the West, but in a western enclave of the East. For a city boy like me, the real West (whatever that is or was) had been incoherently merged with movie mythology and my Red Ryder comic books. Our summer vacations provided the only glimpses I got of the real West. It was like visiting an anthropological zoo spread out over a sizeable portion of the planet, carpeted with sagebrush, partitioned by barbwire. In the more desolate areas, the uninhabited land between ranches was as big as East Coast counties, every man an Adam, every woman an Eve.

Now and then we saw cowboys on their horses tending cows, just like in the movies. We visited open-pit copper mines and ghost towns. We saw Indians selling blankets and jewelry. These sightings were all the proof a young boy needed that the Old West (rather, the Old White West) was still alive and the legends true.

When Dad retired, he and Mom went to Reno for a few days of gambling almost every month. He played blackjack at the $1-minimum-bet tables, and she played the nickel and penny slot machines. This continued until he died.

After Dad's funeral, Mom and I headed south to visit family in California. But our first stop was Reno, and the birth of the family memorial blackjack tournament.

A year before he died, Dad had given me a little card for my wallet, and I kept it there for decades. On it he had written the rules for how not to lose very much money playing blackjack. The rules were intended to minimize the blackjack dealer's enormous advantage: the player has to draw first. If the player exceeds twenty-one, the player loses, no matter what the dealer draws. Dad's rules, which came from an early version of a self-help book, were not the system known as counting. That system, although profitable, is hard work and sucks all the fun out of blackjack. Besides, casinos have developed several measures to thwart counting, including shuffling together as many as six decks at a time. Try counting those.

I was scared to death the first time I sat at the table. Decisions had to be made in front of other players and the dealer. Everyone could see my cards, as they are dealt face up. Under that pressure, it was difficult remembering the rules for not losing much money.

I played until I lost $20. Then I would go play poker slots until I worked up the courage to play another round of blackjack. Eventually, Dad's rules gave me the strength to put up with gamblers who yelled at me because I had asked for an unseen card that caused us to lose. In essence, they were accusing me of being clairvoyant and not using my powers. Gambling is mathematical; gamblers are not.

I moved to the East Coast in the 1960s, and Christmas was the only time I visited the family in Portland. From 1980 to 2001, the year before Mom died, she and I flew to Reno the day after Christmas for two or three days of gambling at the casinos where she and Dad had played.

Rather than marking the passage of time, as annual events want to do, the Reno interludes seemed more like the resumption of something that was always the same, a reassuring constant. It was the one time of year Mom and I had to ourselves, and the only time we had to deepen our relationship as adults. And it was salve for the guilt I felt for moving so far away from home.

When Mom died, so did Reno. It had always been a family thing. I gave the rules to a niece.

Part V.

Writing While Old

For most of us, the mind does not age in the way the body does; it lags behind. I feel like a young man trapped in an old man's body. The reckoning happened about thirty years ago, when a woman I was attracted to wanted to set me up with her mother.

I am old. When my great-grandmother, whom I knew, was born, Ulysses S. Grant was president. Writing has been a great friend during my natural deterioration. I consider myself lucky to have found a voice so near the end.

THE VOICE OF THOSE THAT WEEP

IT HAPPENED WHILE I WAS DOING THE DISHES. It happened because of an odd thing that has come with aging, in a long parade of odd things. The music I listen to has gotten older. Music is important in my life, as it is for most people. In recent years I have become increasingly attracted to music of the Renaissance. In my neck of the world, its fan base is incredibly small. Many of my friends regard it as a harmless but unlistenable personality defect.

Almost all of the music I am passionate about—from the late 1400s to early 1600s—comes from a time of fatalism and poverty, of plague and Inquisition, of common childhood mortality, of dangerous medicine. Aging opened me up to what I think is the purpose of this music: it's a drug for the soul, always ethereal, occasionally ecstatic. The polyphony beckons full engagement. And sometimes the music becomes personal, digging deep into my psyche and soul.

It happened as I listened to the motet *Versa est in luctum*, from a mass for the dead composed by a Spanish priest during the Inquisition. His name is Tomás Luis de Victoria, and he composed some of the most emotionally powerful music I have heard. I had no idea music like this was being written long before Mahler and the Righteous Brothers.

The motet has a hook in it, a slowly pulsating wail about halfway through the four-minute work. As it floats above the mourners, the wail is intensified by its restraint.

It happened even though I had heard the piece a dozen times. As I stood there washing the dishes, the wail came, and I fell to the floor sobbing nearly to suffocation, my body heaving. I had been overcome by the strongest feeling of grief I have ever experienced. I was grieving for everyone I have ever loved who is gone. It was the first time I had openly, passionately grieved for my mother, whose death affected me the most. And I grieved for many friends—too many—among the departed. And I grieved for my father, which was a long time coming.

> *Versa est in luctum cithara mea.* . . . *My harp is turned to mourning,* and my music into the voice of those that weep.

It has become a reminder to love more those who remain.

The Sirens' Song

D URING A CROSSING OF CABOT STRAIT FROM NOVA
Scotia to Newfoundland, I found myself leaning
against the ferry's starboard rail, looking down
about fifty feet to the mildly turbulent waters, a gray sky
overhead. The sea looked deathly cold, but I must have
heard the sirens' song. The notion—without the desire
—that I could throw myself overboard sent a shudder
through body and soul. I considered how no one would
ever know and could only presume I had cast myself adrift.
Not many passengers venture outside on the ferry, and
there were no windows in the adjacent bulkhead. Phase
two of the event would not even begin until the crew went
looking for the driver of the car that was making a bother
on the vehicle deck as other cars departed.

I have felt this shadow of an urge before, usually at
cliff edges, which is why I am afraid of heights, uncertain
whether the fear is of an accidental fall or of potential
irrationality. Why should the thought even occur? Not
jumping should be an elemental instinct, like not looking
at the sun. But I know the partition between jumping and
not jumping can be paper-thin.

Early the next morning, in a Port aux Basques hotel, I
woke up in a state of dread from having even entertained
the notion. I couldn't calm myself until I remembered this
happens to me at edgy heights and was not some new gift
of aging. In recent years I have thought about whether I
would have the courage to stage an early exit if beset by a

terminal and agonizing illness. It is a circumstance I regard as self-euthanasia rather than suicide. But so far, no motive has had standing at the edge of cliffs or ships—only notion, a thrilling concept from the mind's nether region.

How strange is the human capacity for suicide, how strange that evolution would allow such a thing. We all seem to have it, the dark cousin of our noble capacity for self-sacrifice. Maybe it is the cost of that capacity.

Meditations on death have become more frequent as I age, prompted by that old man staring at me from the mirror. Cultured men of the Renaissance began preparing for death at age sixty, summing up their life's work, bringing closure where possible, and smoothing the edges of any contribution that might endure. I have joked with friends that I am way behind, but I haven't even begun to sum up, or close, or smooth. I am unfinished. I have plans.

It is said the mariner dies when the sirens' song ends. For now, they must keep singing.

THE BENCH

NOT UNTIL MOM DIED DID I REALIZE THE SIGNIFICANCE of the place of death. Our culture ritualizes places where lots of people have died at once, like battlefields and plane crash sites. But with few exceptions, the ritualization of the place of death for most of us is a very private matter.

One of those exceptions is the memorialization of highway fatalities by the placement of crosses or floral wreaths off the shoulder at the site of the accident. I started paying attention to these when I lived in sparsely populated Montana in the late 1960s. You could travel beautiful fifty-mile stretches of highway and see nothing of human origin beyond one cluster of knotty pine cabins and maybe three gratuitous highway fatality memorials. There were long, lonely stretches where I saw more memorials than opposing vehicles. I wondered whether, over time, there might be fewer vehicles and more memorials until there was no one left to do the remembering.

Before Mom died, I didn't understand the full significance of these memorials and thought they were rather morbid. She died of ravages related to breast cancer fifteen months after the diagnosis. Like so many other emotional events in my life, I still haven't fully come to terms with it and usually cringe when I think about it.

As death approached, Mom was counseled on her condition by her doctor at the hospital, and she decided to spend her last few days under terminal hospice care at a nursing facility. She was given water but no food and was made to feel as comfortable as possible. It seemed almost but not quite like assisted suicide. Call it assisted natural death.

The facility that my sister and I chose was the second one we visited. The first was an older multifloored institutional-looking building with long stark hallways. The hallway we entered was filled with people in wheelchairs waiting for attention outside an office. Some looked anxious, others seemed dazed. A few looked at us—complete strangers—pleadingly. The hallway reeked of the smell of urine. And this was Portland, Oregon, 2002, a city that prides itself as one of the most humanistic in the nation.

Surely there was a better way for these people to die. A curtain had suddenly been pulled back on something carefully hidden away, of how horribly yet routinely our system, and our families, can treat us when we are no longer able to care for ourselves. Behind the cultural façade, beneath the American hubris, is a nation of smug barbarians. My sister and I left quickly, she in tears, I rigid from horror.

The facility we chose was a modern single-floor building beautifully designed around a courtyard landscaped with trees, flowering shrubs, goldfish pools, paths, bridges, and benches. The large windows in the hospice rooms looked out onto this yard. It was still an institution, but people were being cared for in their rooms, not in a hallway, and there was no smell of urine. After Mom was settled in, we talked awhile and offered to read to her (we would have predicted *Gone with the Wind*), but she gently told us to leave, more a request than an order. I think she said it to spare us the agony of waiting for her to die while in her presence, and maybe sparing herself some agony as well. My sister and I came back and visited with her a few times every day during the three days before she died. But I have occasionally felt some guilt for not having stayed by her bedside, for not being there at the end. "Her family was at her bedside when she died." That appears in so many obituaries, but can it be so often true? Is the family sitting there day and night? No playing cards in the cafeteria? No sitting in the kitchen waiting for the phone to ring? Death can take its time.

After one of our visits while she was still alive, I walked out into that beautiful garden in the courtyard and sat on the bench facing her room. I have been holding on to that moment ever since. It was here that all my love and guilt came together, as I looked into the room where Mom was dying. And I wondered whether I would ever have the strength to come back here and sit again.

The hospice where Mom died is not far from my sister's house in Portland and is on a major street. When I visit once or twice a year, we usually pass by it, without comment. My sister must pass by it at least weekly, and I imagine she has grown used to it. But not I. Every time we pass the hospice, I am silently overwhelmed by those emotions I felt on the bench at the place of death. It is my quiet memorial. It has more meaning for me than her grave.

Now I understand those roadside crosses and wreaths. If there is anything beyond this life, the places where they left us are the portals.

THE GAME IS ON

THE DRUG CARTEL'S HIT MAN IN THE FILM *NO COUNTRY for Old Men* is a powerful and mythical evocation of Death. He brings to mind a similar characterization in Ingmar Bergman's film *The Seventh Seal*. In both movies, Death loves to engage his victims before consummation, sometimes with game playing, sometimes with droll and very dark humor. He loves playing the game, even though he knows he will ultimately win. In *The Seventh Seal*, he agrees to the knight's delaying tactic, a game of chess. In *No Country*, he plays a game of chance with the convenience store proprietor. The proprietor correctly calls the coin toss, but all he wins is a reprieve—or in Death's word, "Everything."

As a young man I was fascinated by allegorical treatments of death, but not much threatened by them. It was only a movie, a novel, a poem. I was well buffered by the actuary's tables. But now I am in my eighties on a trail blazed with abandoned body parts. The bell tolls, the game is on.

Chess is an apt metaphor. The player requires new strategies to compensate for each lost attribute. Death is a relentless adversary.

My mother was an extraordinarily calm and gentle woman. I know precisely the times she got angry, and even then her anger may have been acting (but very good acting). Those angry times were when she had to impose corporal punishment on a bad little boy. Corporal punishment was a popular and acceptable corrective in those times.

Our house was heated by a wood furnace in the basement, which was reached by a set of stairs that descended from the kitchen. Whenever I committed a punishable offense, Mom would angrily but silently go to the kitchen and descend the stairs. My heart filled with terror as my body, against all will and common sense, was pulled by unseen forces into the kitchen. Before she got to the last step of her descent, I was already bawling and pleading, "No, Mom! No!"

In the basement she went to the woodpile and selected a piece of kindling. "Richard James LeBlond, you get down here right now." Normally calling me Dick, it was the only time she ever used my formal and middle names, the courtroom judge about to administer sentence. "You get down here right now or else." I didn't know what "or else" was, but I knew it was better not to know. So I would start down the stairs slowly, my legs heavy with reluctance. When I got to the basement floor (a journey that in retrospect seems more painful than the ass whomping) she put her hand on my shoulder and turned my body into position.

"Get your hands out of the way or I will hit them too." Her intention was to improve my behavior, and it worked.

But now that she is gone, along with some of my improvement (and the few body parts), I am learning that her lesson has another use. I am able to willfully descend the stairs unaided toward that doctor standing there with a piece of kindling in his hand, in the form of a flesh probe or its consequence, a biopsy result. (The difference here is that the punishment from aging is gratuitous rather than corrective.)

It was a late November afternoon when I returned
home from the second thyroid biopsy, at the beginning
of that dreadful interval between summation and verdict.
Leaf fall had exposed the dark trunks of the trees towering
above the house. They looked more sullen than gaunt. The
lives of deciduous trees continue unnoticed beneath the
seasonal subterfuge. Maybe they trick Death into missing
an appointment.

Home is comfort's bastion, but the biopsy had exposed
its fragility. I allowed a momentary return of foreboding
and then, in a surge of life force, decided to do some yard
work in preparation for spring. Right then and there, in
the dawning dusk. Death of course will win, but for a
while at least, it can be outplayed.

WRITING WHILE OLD

FOR MOST OF US, LIFE IS NOT SHORT WHEN WE'RE young. There is plenty of time to waste, and we take our share. But when you reach your eighties (which, as an ex-smoker, I incorrectly presumed was beyond my grasp), life is decidedly short and getting shorter.

In my decrepitude, I have increasingly found myself compelled to write about aging. As the edge nears, all is fair game. I have written about the deaths of loved ones, about biopsies and discarded body parts. I have written about self-euthanasia and adult diapers. Someone may benefit from knowing that an unpleasant experience or thought is shared, that it is part of a common, if largely unspoken, humanity. I am obliged to address what comes my way. Writing is the therapy.

Old people talking about their medical adventures long ago achieved the majority needed to become a legitimate stereotype. It is probably what the elders talked about in front of the cave as they softened leather with their gums. I don't like talking to friends and relatives about my medical adventures. Nonetheless, I still have urges to pass along what I have learned, especially from the biopsy experience, and I have been doing that as a writer. In other words, I don't like talking about my medical adventures unless I can tell the whole world.

Today I am in that dreadful interval between the biopsy and its secret. I have endured several, running the diagnostic gamut from noncancerous to precancerous (oops!

there goes the thyroid) to cancerous (oops! there goes the prostate). I appreciate that most of me is still living. And as a late-blooming writer, I treasure what seems sufficient clarity, writing as far as I can toward the end of days, admittedly trying to forge a readable immortality.

I have a team of medical professionals committed to this dream. Ethnically, it is a diverse group, probably due to our proximity to a large military installation. My pulmonary specialist is from the Philippines, my urologist is African American, my proctologist and endocrinologist are Middle Eastern, and my periodontist is Panamanian.

It is my prostate biopsy I want to talk about, and that was performed by the urologist. If mine are the measure, biopsies are not pleasant. They involve needles, knives, pincers, and probes. Even if most of the pain is prevented, they can be very uncomfortable. The prostate biopsy was very, very uncomfortable. It felt like the urologist had mistaken my butt for a parking garage and had driven his SUV into it. He backed in and out of twelve different parking spaces, taking a snippet of prostate at each one. There was never any nerve pain, but the discomfort was so strong I eventually passed out.

And now we have come to what this essay is really about: the conversation the urologist was having with his nurse as he maneuvered his SUV through my abdomen. The conversation was relaxed and cordial, as if we were enjoying espressos and coffee cakes, as if one of us were not at the outer edge of his sanity. They were talking about Plato and Socrates.

"You know," said the urologist, "I really don't think it was fair of Plato to attribute his most controversial ideas to Socrates."

A tiny part of me wanted to laugh—not because I thought the statement was funny but because of the circumstantial absurdity. The larger part of me chose to pass out instead, which was the proper response. Ever since, I have regarded this incongruous yet almost mystical moment as a cosmic gift given to the wrong person. It was intended for a novelist. Vonnegut. Dostoyevsky. But it became part of the inspiration that eventually got me to take responsibility as a writer for what comes my way—as, according to the urologist, Plato should have done.

I have the lungs of an ex-smoker, and sometimes I wheeze, often in the morning after a day outdoors. Once the wheezing was so faint that at first I thought it was the call of a distant flight of geese, the dark parody of a favorite sound. The old man rues the image, but it is cherished by the writer. Poetry, the soul's shorthand, inhabits even (or especially) the darkest metaphors.

WRITING ON SAND

PROVINCETOWN HAS BEEN A DESTINATION FOR ARTISTS and writers since the late 1800s. I moved there in the 1970s hoping to become a writer, without realizing hope had nothing to do with it. In the early twentieth century the town had nurtured writers like John Dos Passos, Louise Bryant, Jack Reed, Edmund Wilson, and Eugene O'Neill. The first-ever production of an O'Neill play, *Bound East for Cardiff,* happened on a Provincetown wharf in 1916.

When I came to the bipolar town—serene in winter, madhouse in summer—Pulitzer-winning poets Mary Oliver and Stanley Kunitz were living there. Gregory Corso, the first Beat poet to be published, could regularly be seen in a Commercial Street bar, even during the day. There always seemed to be an empty stool next to him, but I never had the nerve to sit on it. Whenever I passed by, I couldn't help but look at him through the open door. Along with the other Beats, Corso was like a religious relic.

But in that era, the local literary elephant was Norman Mailer. Although Mailer was a resident of New York City, he spent a good part of every year in Provincetown, where he owned a house. And now he spends all year there, in the cemetery. Provincetown had (and still has) his heart. I eventually encountered him a few times in casual social situations, but the tiny incident I am relating here involves a time before then, when he was just one of the world's foremost authors.

In the summer of 1975 the two of us lived in separate apartments in the same waterfront house, he on the second floor, with me on the first floor directly below. Either he had not yet bought his house, or it was being used for another purpose, maybe by one of his several ex-wives, who wouldn't let him in.

At the time, I was doing my best to act like a writer but really wasn't producing much more than bad haiku, which is surprisingly easy to do. And the time I spent in the apartment became a nightmare, because Mailer was assiduously applying himself upstairs, writing daily and at length, exposing the sham of my pretensions.

Although his obituary said he eschewed the typewriter and wrote by hand, he was prolifically typing something overhead, probably a submission manuscript. And the endless tap-tap-tap had the same effect as Chinese water torture in the apartment below, driving me out into the streets of Provincetown until the wee hours of the morning.

It took decades for me to accept that I was not going to be the writer I wanted to be. I wish I could say it was Mailer's fault, but like hope, he had nothing to do with it. Not until after I retired as a biologist did I find, or become comfortable with, my own voice.

The epiphany came as I sat on a toilet in, fittingly, Provincetown, where I was visiting a friend. She kept a pile of literature on the commoner's think tank behind me. In the pile was a catalog of courses for Campus Provincetown, a by-the-seat-of-your-pants education effort so typical of that town.

Among the offered courses was one titled "Creating Conditions for Flow," on overcoming artistic blocks. The brief description said, "When you are in 'flow,' you are highly productive and intensely concentrated on your work—so much so that you may lose all track of time. In flow, your inner critic is silent."

That last phrase produced the eureka moment. I saw the inner critic for the stifling tyrant he was. He remains one of the voices in my head, but now must wait his turn.

THE TWEED COAT

IT HAS BEEN SAID THAT QUITTING HEROIN IS EASIER THAN quitting tobacco. If that is true, then as an ex-smoker I can say that giving up either is a piece of cake compared to the addiction of the publishing junkie. After the rush of that first acceptance, there is no turning back.

My dealer is a website that opens its tweed coat (with leather elbow patches) to reveal a list pinned to the silk lining. It is a list of literary journals and magazines currently seeking submissions of poems, short stories, and creative nonfiction.

In the beginning, my dealer was a website that lists its wares alphabetically. I soon realized I would die long before I got to the journal *ZYZZYVA*, or the journal itself would be dead. The founders of *ZYZZYVA* must have known they'd end up at the bottom of alphabetized lists, willing to paint themselves into the darkest corner because they didn't want to hear from writers who go through lists alphabetically.

Then I discovered the "calls for submission" websites, and my addiction became hard-wired. Here were journals with open submission periods fresh off the boat from Columbia or tunneled in from Mexico.

Do I have something they might be interested in? I read the editor's credo. I'm an essayist, so I head for the creative nonfiction. This is where I am usually thwarted. Most creative nonfiction in literary journals is what is referred to as *narrative* nonfiction. It would be mistaken

for fiction were it not for the label. That's not how I write.
But I do employ tiny bits of fiction to avoid beatings and
lawsuits. A lot of what passes for fiction is memoir in a
witness protection program.

(*Storyscape Journal*'s mission statement on the need to
declare whether something is fiction or true: "It totally
matters if it's true or invented, because I need to know
if I should run around screaming based on the information you gave me or just imagine myself running around
screaming.")

Essays are the stepchild of most literary journals, trail-
ing behind the beloved poems, short stories, and fiction-
iferous narrative nonfiction. It is a generous journal that
allows space for an essay or two. Inspired invention has
priority over inspired observation, with narrative nonfiction
somewhere in between.

I wade through the website list one by one, looking
for connection and suitability. The submission itself is
anything but submissive. It is exposure, the thrill of risk,
all or nothing. The numerous rejections intensify the few
acceptances and keep in check the excesses of ego.

Even the acceptance comes with a reality check. When
I see a journal calling for submissions after it has published my essay, I feel like I have been dumped. I know it
was just a one-night stand; still, I gave her my heart. But
she has moved on, having her own addiction to attend to.

As every junkie knows, the fix is ephemeral. It is only
days, or hours, before I return to the tweed coat, to the
quest for the next fix. Payment is a little piece of my soul.
Bit by bit the tweed coat acquires majority interest, and the
moment of no return goes unnoticed.

A FAILURE TO WRITE

TRAGIC EVENTS OFTEN CHANGE THE LIVES OF SURVIVORS. Some become part of the team raising money to find a cancer cure. Others rally against drunk drivers, or lobby on behalf of safer air travel. Survivor guilt is often involved in these life changes, but I'm sure most people are also inspired by the higher motive of not letting the victim or victims die in vain. The survivor feels a responsibility, even an obligation, to set things right.

For nearly forty years I was burdened by that obligation because I was unable to fulfill it, from a failure to write. One day in Athens, Greece, in the mid-1970s, I witnessed hundreds of men and women holding hands and marching unarmed toward the sound of automatic weapon fire—that is, the sound of carnage—during an uprising under the military dictatorship of Colonel Georgios Papadopoulos.

It was one of several traumatic events I witnessed or endured during two and a half years in southern Europe and North Africa. The trip started as an open-ended vacation, but by the time it was over, I had spent a day surrounded by Moroccan police armed with submachine guns; sat in a Guardia Civil interrogation room convinced I would be sentenced to six years and a day in a Spanish prison; befriended an American who against his will had become a pig inspector in Yugoslavia; then had my own encounter with Athens's secret police. And for a while I worked for a newspaper that was likely financed by the CIA.

I returned to the States in 1974 full of these incredible stories, but it took me nearly forty years to write them. I lacked confidence. More than once I told myself I was a second-rate writer with a third-rate mind. During that long interim, I kept hearing the voices of the Athens marchers and knew their story might die with me if I couldn't set it down. In all those years, I was never able to find another account of what I had witnessed.

I had written a brief op-ed piece about the marchers back in 2002, but I still needed to write the whole story. By the winter of 2010, I realized I would have to write it whether I was ready or not. Nearly seventy years old and thirteen years into my COPD, I had to assume I was running out of time. And I wanted to relate all of my Mediterranean adventures, or at least as many as I could squeeze past my inner censor. Some things happened others don't need to know about, and there is embarrassment enough in what the censor allowed.

February 2010 was a good time to be indoors. Thanks to the closing window of opportunity, I had reached a truce with my demons (aka inner critic), and out poured the stories. I wrote nonstop, six to seven days a week, eight to ten hours a day for two months. I began each day listening to the same piece of music, during my morning walk, a ten-minute-long *Salve Regina* written in the 1500s by a Spanish priest during the Inquisition. It set the perfect mood, as my journey had begun among the *gitanos* on the south coast of Spain.

During the decades of not writing, I had told my stories several times to friends, which helped to keep details alive. Even so, I had forgotten a few names, and I'm fairly certain one character was actually two. But the stories remained clear, and I can still experience their actuality in my mind. That is especially true of the Athens marchers.

Hemingway said, "The first draft of anything is shit."

But for me the first draft became another level of inspiration, and I wrote with a greater sense of responsibility, propelled by the marchers. Every time I came to their passage during rewrites, I bawled from reliving the experience. Even now, I bawl when I read that passage. It is my own little post-traumatic stress disorder.

The task of writing and rewriting was like working at a four-dimensional loom. The first draft was the warp, and it became a process of adding on and pulling out, of modifying forms and hues. The rewriting process brought new insights and taught me how to let go of that which had dulled.

Even my inner critic was happy.

ACKNOWLEDGMENTS

Essays in *Homesick for Nowhere* were previously published in the following journals:

"Homesick for Nowhere" *High Country News: Writers on the Range*, 2017.
"The Appalling Mountain" *Blueline Literary Magazine*, 2016.
"Too Long Tea" *Hippocampus*, 2015.
"Eating America" *Woodhall Press: Flash Nonfiction Food anthology*, 2020.
"An Advanced Human Being" *Carbon Culture Review*, 2015.
"Tea with the Grizzlies" *Cirque*, 2014.
"Riding in the Back with Killer" *Wanderlust Journal*, 2018.
"Let's Restore the Draft" *Smoky Blue Literary and Arts Magazine*, 2017.
"Alternative Definitions" *The Offbeat*, 2018.
"In an Okinawa Kitchen" *Sisyphus Magazine*, 2021.
"Lesson at the Feeder" *Split Rock Review*, 2017.
"Amphibious Assault" *Zoomorphic*, 2016.
"Sand Lovers" *Kudzu House*, 2015.
"Bigfoot" *Zoomorphic*, 2017.
"Rooming with a Weasel" *Split Rock Journal*, 2018.
"The Natural Moment" *Visitant Literary Journal*, 2017.
"Rough at the Edges" *Split Rock Journal*, 2017.
"Trespassing for Fun and Profit" *Split Rock Journal*, 2018.
"Curse of the Alewives" *little somethings press*, 2019.
"Alice's Rock" *little somethings press*, 2020.
"Ancient Urge" *Humana Obscura*, 2021.
"Just a Cat" *Foliate Oak*, 2015.
"Spellbinding Monotony" *Cagibi*, 2018.
"Dead Phones for Dwayne" *Cagibi*, 2018
"From the Found Journal of Captain Miles Standish" *Poor Yorick*, 2021.
"A Strange Thing from the Deep" *Concis*, 2017.
"Dorian at the Doryman" *Wanderlust Journal*, 2020.
"At Last, a Drinking and Dining Guide to the North Sydney Waterfront" *Wanderlust Journal*, 2018.
"Too Loud To Be Forlorn" *Ruminate*, 2020.
"The Codroy Cobblestones" *Concis*, 2016.
"The Ugly Stick" *Ruminate*, 2020.
"Fluffing Dark Tickle" *Main Street Rag: Of Burgers and Barrooms anthology*, 2017.
"Would You Like a Parable with Your Coffee?" *Cagibi*, 2018.
"Fisherman's Brewis – Almost Edible" *Stained Pages Press*, 2015
"Ghost in the Attic" *Newfoundland Quarterly*, 2020.
"I Eat a Sea Mammal" *Lowestoft Chronicle*, 2016.
"Gutting Turbits" *Aji Magazine*, 2015.
"A Bear Ponders My Edibility" *Appalachia*, 2016.
"Duel on the Strait" *Jonah Magazine*, 2015.
"An Essay in Which Pam Greer Oozes Out of Her Clothes" *Alimentum Journal*, 2015.
"From Snitch to Scab" *bioStories*, 2017.
"A Beautiful Lie" *Sky Island*, 2018.
"Elvis" *Hobart*, 2019.
"Touching God" *New Theory*, 2016 (as "Fleetwood Rising").
"Mentor of Cool" *River Teeth*, 2017.
"The Man inside the Effigy" *Burningword*, 2021.
"Going to Hell with Laurel and Hardy" *Crux Magazine*, 2020.
"American Timbuktu" *Wanderlust Journal*, 2019.

"The Voice of Those That Weep" *Stories of Music anthology*, 2015.

"The Siren's Song" *Smoky Blue Literary and Arts Magazine*, 2016.

"The Bench" *Medical Literary Messenger*, 2016.

"Writing While Old" *Trampset*, 2018.

"The Game Is On" *Chaleur Magazine*, 2018.

"Writing on Sand" *South 85 Writers Blog*, 2014.

"The Tweed Coat" *South 85 Writers Blog*, 2015.

"A Failure to Write" *South 85 Writers Blog*, 2016.

ABOUT THE AUTHOR

RICHARD LEBLOND is a retired biologist living in North Carolina. His essays and photographs have appeared in numerous U.S. and international journals, including *Montreal Review, Redux, Compose, Trampset,* and *Still Point Arts Quarterly.*

Like every other English lit graduate in 1966, LeBlond wanted to write the Great American Novel. It took four decades before he realized that wasn't going to happen. A nature lover, he joined the National Park Service during the interim, working first at Glacier National Park in Montana, then on to Cape Cod National Seashore. Still in pursuit of that novel, he rode the wave of young Americans heading to Europe in 1972, coming back home two years later with a bag full of stories that stayed in the bag when he returned to Cape Cod as an environmental activist, turning his knack for identifying wild plants, which became an obsession, into a career. Moving to North Carolina in 1990, he went to work for the state as a field biologist. As retirement approached seventeen years later, he wondered whether he might have the courage to open that now-huge bag of stories he had been lugging around.

He did. This is his first book.

CPSIA information can be obtained
at www.ICGtesting.com
Printed in the USA
LVHW052103110523
746750LV00003B/558